The Countryman Gardening Book

THE COUNTRYMAN BOOK OF RESCUING THE PAST
THE COUNTRYMAN WILDLIFE BOOK
THE COUNTRYMAN ANIMAL BOOK

The Countryman Gardening Book

Compiled by D. MACER WRIGHT

DAVID & CHARLES : NEWTON ABBOT

Set in 11/13 point Plantin
and printed in Great Britain
by Ebenezer Baylis and Son Limited
The Trinity Press Worcester and London
for David & Charles (Holdings) Limited
South Devon House Newton Abbot Devon

Contents

Winter

CONTENTS

List of Illustrations

PLATES

IN TEXT

What a man needs in gardening is a cast-iron back with a hinge in it.

C. D. Warner

Introduction

The compiler of 'Other Men's Flowers' is happily free from the restraints of modesty. He can blow trumpet notes loud and clear, for the trumpet is not his own. In fact he has at his disposal as many of those glorious instruments as he has contributors to his collection. But to blow each one would be an exhausting business, so I will content myself by proclaiming that this collection of gardening articles from *The Countryman* cannot fail to please, entertain and inform all who follow the noble art of making things grow.

Its gathering has been a delightful task, but one not without its moments of melancholy, for much that I would have included had my brief run to two books has had to be omitted in order to keep within the confines of one book. I can claim to have been presented with the compiler's most difficult job, which is to select from material of universal excellence.

To resolve the problem, I have limited each author to one contribution; in fact this is not a complete resolution because some authors have written many articles for the magazine, and to choose from these has been an assignment in itself. But at least this strict discipline has assured the widest possible representation of writers.

Sometimes we shall find mention of the same plants by different people; this is inevitable in a book of this nature, but it does not mean mere repetition, for each person has something of his or her own to say.

Not all the plants mentioned are easily obtainable; I have ranged over some forty years of *The Countryman*, and fashions and foibles change. However, there are nurserymen who keep a nucleus of old favourites for gardeners who do not readily submit to the dictates of fashion.

I have followed the original pattern of the seasons, but apart from that, chronology has given way to informality. I wanted a deck chair and bedside kind of book, to be opened anywhere at any time of day or night, a mixture of the serious and light hearted, punctuated here and there by some of the best garden verse of our time.

Very occasionally I have strayed outside the immediate confines of the garden into fields and woods, and once among wheat, but always with an eye to the companionship of the wild with the cultivated.

Finally, a Tail Corn to end each season shows that gardening has its humorists. The humour is unconscious, or at any rate unprofessional, which is usually the choicest kind.

D. MACER WRIGHT

SPRING

MIMOSA

I planted there a wisp of feathery grey,
And waited, seven years of nights and days;
And now before my door there shining stands
A bee cathedral, thunderous with praise.

Fenella Boyle

REMINDER OF A FRIEND   Bernard Gill

Every year a miracle seems to happen just inside our gate. A plant glowing with health and beauty rises out of the gravel at the base of the few massed slabs of magnesian limestone that we call the rockery. It is dwarf in habit, and few passers-by give it a second glance. Yet for delicacy of form and purity of colour its flowers are among the loveliest of spring.

For nine months of the year it hides underground. Then, one day in March, a few grains of gravel are lifted and pushed aside by the point of a furled brown leaf. Soon this pioneer is joined by several more, and the leaves unroll and expand to show a dusky green surface, prettily mottled with splashes of purple-brown. Then the flower-buds appear as a cluster of two or three pendent pearls. Even when in full bloom they still hang their heads, though the petals, which are now rosy, are brushed back, exposing the stamens.

This paragon of April flowers grows from a long narrow white bulb which looks like a canine tooth; hence its name, dog's-tooth violet. But why violet, which it resembles in neither colour nor shape? It is, in fact, a lily.

Our 'tooth' was given to us by a friend many years ago. We planted it incredulously, hardly believing that anything would come of it. Yet our lack of faith was put to shame the following spring, and since then the plant has never failed us. It does not increase, nor does it diminish; it steadfastly survives, braving the perils of changeable weather. Last year it was buried under a snowdrift when in full bloom, but it came up bright and shining when its icy covering melted away.

Year after year it appears as March goes out, lifts its marbled leaves and rosy flowers above the cold ground, displays its fragile beauty for a few weeks and dies down, leaving no sign of its presence.

But it has kept alive the memory of a friend.

OLD FASHIONED PRIMROSES   Eda D. Hume

The old double primroses are now mainly found in old-fashioned gardens, where they are usually cared for by someone who likes to make a collection, and will buy or exchange to add to it. Those most easy to obtain are the Double White; the variety called by our grandmothers the 'evening primrose' (*Primula lilacina plena*);* Marie Crousse, of Continental origin; and A. De Moulin.

The gem of the doubles is Madame Pompadour, a lovely velvety red, and the next is Old Salmon. There are at least four yellows; Early and Late Sulphur, Cloth of Gold and Carter's Cloth of Gold. In the reds we have Crimson King; *sanguinea plena*, with a white line edge, called 'Red Paddy'; and the all-red variety usually known as Scotch Red. Then there is a double blue, which is very hard to obtain, and two French greys—Dingy and another, a blush varying according to soil, which I believe to be the same as *carnea plena*. Rose du Barri explains itself. Burgundy is wine-purple; as is Amaranth, which is, I think, the same as *purpurea*. There was an Old Cream, but I cannot say if this still exists. All the family frequently grow long, woody rootstocks. When dividing, these may be cut off and pieces of them replanted. They will sprout leaves and make new plants, and the original one will make better roots after the woody part has been removed. All these double primroses are delightfully perfumed.

More common than the old doubles are the Bon Accords,

---

* The true evening primrose does not belong to the primrose family, *Primulaceae* but to the Willow-Herb family, *Onagraceae*, and to the genus *Oenothera*. There are several species, the most common being *O biennis*, sometimes reaching 5ft in height. Various cultivated hybrids occur, some small enough for the rock garden.

a

b

c

d

Old Fashioned Primroses

(*a*) Bon Accord   (*b*) *Primula lilacina plena*
(*c*) Hose-in-hose   (*d*) Jack-in-the-Green

descended from a plant of A. De Moulin, which Cocker found in the gardens of Lord Ventry in Kerry. He took it to Scotland and named it from the motto of his native city, Aberdeen. There are now about fifteen varieties of Bon Accord.

Of the single primroses, a very old and early white, Harbinger, seems to have faded into oblivion, but Miss Massey is still to be had; when true, it would be hard to find anything better than its glowing velvety red. Belvedere is the single form of the double *lilacina plena*. There is a green single like an ordinary primrose, and another with pointed petals, each with a rib underneath, as down the centre of a leaf; in his 'Paradisus' (1629), Parkinson called it 'welted'. He illustrated a double green primrose, but described only that with welted petals. No other is known today.

It is still possible to obtain the duplex or hose-in-hose varieties, so called because they resembled 'the dress men doe wear' in Parkinson's day. Were it not for his descriptions and prints, we should know little of these favourites of long ago. The best known is Orange Prince, a little larger than most of the others and of a light yellow; it has a deep, starry, orange eye. Lady Dora, also yellow, is the next in size, with more tubular blossoms. These two are distinctly primrose forms, while Canary Bird and Erin's Gem throw a polyanthus stem, much as do the Bon Accord doubles. Lady Molly is a deep pink, Lady Lettice, usually the favourite of the hose-in-hose family, is cream, edged (or rather shaded) with pink. Maureen is a cream. The reds are represented by Sparkler, the brightest, crimson scarlet; Old Vivid, a little larger, with more yellow in the eye; and Ashfort, brownish red.

The Clown is a striped hose-in-hose. Jackanapes, called by Parkinson a polyanthus, has duplex blossoms larger and flatter than the hose-in-hose. There are several colours, the lower petals being striped with green. When there was a tuft of small leaves growing on the stalk under the blossom, Parkinson called it Jackanapes-on-Horseback, or the foolish or frantic cowslip. With Jack-in-the-Green the points of the sections of the calyx develop into little leaves, as the drawing shows. Plain and curled Gallygaskins are single primroses with calyces enlarged and welted; they may be of any colour, but are mostly orange or yellow.

The double and duplex primroses do not ripen seed. One must obtain pollen from the flowers, apply it to single forms, and again save the seed; then one may be rewarded by a double. Those which are obtained do not seem very lasting. The late Dr McWatt was successful in raising doubles, but eventually lost them all, as I lost some which he gave me. The pollen from double primroses is difficult to obtain; as many as thirty blossoms may be stripped of their petals without yielding any. I do not know whether it is easier to get pollen from the hose-in-hose; the only new one I have heard of or seen was a blue, and I fancy that it no longer exists.

Of the single polyanthuses the rarest are the two old Irish ones; the Quaker and the Quakeress. The first is ice-blue, with a white eye and an even edge of white; there is a faint touch of green in the blue. The other is magenta, with the same white eye and edge. Radiant is a dark, almost black, polyanthus with a small, solid-looking blossom, powdered as it were with gold. Red Indian is a fringed red and yellow, and there is a distinct frilly yellow.

The old growers of polyanthuses in the 1870s showed them in pots and pans, as single plants or in classes of four. Often they were named after the grower; Bullock's Lancer, Pearson's Alexander, Piggott's Duchess of Kent and Buck's George the Fourth; the last seems to have been a favourite. I would like to compare these with our modern polyanthuses, but the only two old ones that remain are the gold-laced varieties, Captain Jones (almost black-centred) and Saturn (dark-crimson); both have perfect rings of gold to edge them.

There are also polyanthuses called Feathers, with ragged, twisted petals. I lost the only one I have seen when all my primroses succumbed to an attack of an aphis which one requires a magnifying glass to see. Unfortunately I was away from home, so it went ahead unchecked; few even of the ordinary bedding polyanthuses were saved. When the leaves turn brown and dry up, drought is usually thought to be the cause; but if the plant is lifted in the earlier stages, and a magnifying glass is used, a minute grey-green aphis will be seen on the woody stock. Permanganate of potash, fairly strong, appears to lay them low, but, even when the plants have been washed and removed to new ground, the attack seems to be renewed, and it might be wiser to use naphthalene or some similar deterrent. The leaves also turn yellow from a grub which makes a hole up the woody stock or stem; this should be followed up, and the stem cut off and burned. Sometimes a family is found at the top of the boring.

Yellow clay is often recommended for these primroses, but we need to go back to the conditions in which they once flourished; the herbaceous border of long ago, mulched in autumn with well-rotted mixed manure (with plenty of leaf-mould in it), and again in early summer, to conserve moisture. The clumps should be divided only when they become too large; once in three years is enough. I am not satisfied that peat is a substitute for leaf-mould. Though primroses do well in the boggy counties of Ireland, I have grown them to perfection where there were no bogs, and no 'turf' was sold.

A FLUTTER OF DOVES   Evelyn Bristowe

As my brother arrived at an age when some boys (and he was one) can briefly sing with the purity of archangels, my mother summoned the organist from a nearby village to instruct him in 'O for the Wings of a Dove'. This family item came back to me as I began to write of *Davidia*, the dove tree, for it was the same brother who, after an immense chasm of years, urged me to plant one. He described its extraordinary romantic beauty at flowering time, when a flock of white doves seem to have alighted on the branches (see picture on page 19). Now that I had more ground, he said, I must order without delay. It is not the unremarkable flowers gracefully suspended from claret-pink stalks that make one think of doves—more utilitarian types are reminded of men's handkerchiefs flopping from breast-pockets—it is the two, or occasionally three, large creamy-white bracts falling over them and coming to wing-like points that have given the tree its popular name. One bract is always much longer than the other, sometimes reaching a length of nine inches.

The dove tree is a native of central and western China, where it was first discovered in 1869 by a Jesuit missionary-botanist Père Armand David. He seems to have done nothing practical about his amazing find, and it was not until 1897 that another missionary Père Farges, collected thirty-seven seeds and dispatched them to Maurice Vilmorin, a nurseryman in France. Only one germinated, after two years; but, following this lax start, it must have grown at tremendous speed, for W. J. Bean records that it flowered in May 1906. Meanwhile a famous firm of nurserymen, Veitch's, had financed E. H. Wilson's first expedition to China in 1899–1902. Although he sent back thousands of *Davidia* seeds, none germinated and they were thrown on a rubbish heap in disgust. Presently, to everyone's complete surprise, small plants sprang up as thickly as mustard and cress, and the supply of vegetative doves was assured. The first of these plants flowered (again according to Bean) in 1911 at Veitch's Combe Wood nurseries at Kingston Hill. H. G. Hillier, a distinguished and debonair latter-day Veitch, tells me that he had this story from Wilson himself as they walked round his Winchester nurseries. His father Edwin Hillier bought what is now his largest *Davidia*—about 40ft high and 30ft across—at Veitch's sale in 1913, when the lease of Combe Wood came to an end. It was in the garden of a Victorian mansion adjoining the one-time Veitch territory that my brother saw the tree so enthusiastically described to me.

The dove tree is deciduous. Because of its poise and exquisite habit it should be treated as a special feature. It rises to a pinnacle and sweeps majestically wide at the base. For this reason it is a great pity, at any rate in its earlier years, to turn it into a standard; much grace is lost, and the doves can no longer flutter to the ground. It is winter-hardy all over the British Isles, for it ripens its wood in the autumn and does not start into growth until late in the spring. It is accommodating as to soil but does best in deep moist loam. The hotter the summer, the more doves there will be the following May. A sunny sheltered position is the ideal choice, for though the immaculate foliage can stand a great deal of punishment, the bracts turn brown in gale-force winds. The leaves are slenderly heart-shaped and a particularly delightful fresh green; the neat serrated edges and intricate veining give the impression of careful pleating. The fruits or seeds look rather like dangling elongated walnuts. They are extremely hard, and the practice nowadays is to stratify them in damp sand for a year, or even two, before planting. They can be speeded up by careful filing or with acid, but neither method should be tried without expert advice.

There is only one species, *D involucrata*. The leaves are silkily hirsute above, and pale and downy beneath. Its variety *vilmoriniana* has smooth leaves but is otherwise roughly identical. Small variations occur in both the species and the variety. Examples are to be found in all arboreta of merit and more important gardens. Tucked away at Royal Lodge in the south-east corner of Windsor Great Park is one of which King George VI was particularly proud and fond.

My dove tree arrived in 1960 as a sturdy three-footer. It grew at once without fuss, though it is true that I hung solicitously over it with watering cans for the first two years. Seven years later it had reached to about 14ft.

'Next year,' I told Mr Hillier, 'I expect flowers.'

'Give it another five years,' he said, 'you'll just be in your prime.'

'More likely in a bath-chair,' I said, rather put out. 'I shall scatter bone meal and rely on Bean.'

If you are young, plant beautiful trees and go on planting them as long as you have room. I know of a couple well over eighty who spend happy days, weeks, even months deciding where to place some new treasure. Perhaps that is why they have reached their present ages. Certainly it will be a good way to remember them long after they have gone.

VIBURNUMS IN A CHILTERN GARDEN Maisie Fitter

Nothing gives me greater pleasure in late May than to take an unsuspecting visitor, who is being 'shown the garden', round the yew hedge and confront him with *Viburnum tomentosum* Lanarth in full flower (see picture on page 19). Seven feet high and twice as wide, it is a magnificent sight; a mass of pure white, large, flat, clustered flowers on short stiff stems, crowding all along the spreading branches, in close-packed tiers from the top right down to the ground. Each flower-head has an inner cluster of tiny fertile florets surrounded by an outer ring of larger sterile ones, which gives it the attractive lace-cap appearance. But it is the mass effect that is so staggering and invariably provokes admiring cries, so that I can bask in just a little reflected glory—without, of course, any justification at all. No tree in the garden gets less attention; yet every year without fail, for nearly a month, it flowers with the same profusion. A viburnum of this size needs space, and the dark background of the yew hedge is the perfect foil for it. It also makes a fine specimen tree in the middle of a lawn, where its attractive shape and growth can be appreciated. In the autumn it gives another splendid display, this time of deep rich red leaves. It is among the first of the trees and shrubs in our Chiltern garden to turn, in early September or even late August, the only ones to get in ahead of it being two other varieties of *V tomentosum*; and it usually retains its leaves until November. Surprisingly this early autumn colouring is not at all depressing, perhaps because the leaves change to deep claret without any trace of the tawny oranges and yellows one associates with autumn.

The Japanese snowball tree, *V tomentosum plicatum*, though smaller, flowers about the same time and has the characteristic spreading growth of the species. Its flowers resemble those of the common snowball tree, which is the sterile garden form of our native guelder-rose and may grow to 15ft in height. The Japanese tree will not exceed 9ft or 10ft, and ours shows no sign of even approaching that. The tight 'snowballs' are composed of pure white, sterile flowers. Perhaps more attractive still are the larger flowers of the variety, *V tp grandiflorum*, for they are a rich cream tinted with pink (see picture on page 20).

One of the better and more accommodating viburnums, the hybrid semi-evergreen *V burkwoodii*, flowers rather earlier. It makes a shapely upstanding bush, 7ft or 8ft high, with dark shining leaves; and in early spring it becomes a mass of tightly clustered, rounded flower-heads, white flushed pink; the buds too are pink. It is worth planting near a window, or in a place you pass regularly, for its most delicious scent. We have one bush on a corner of the house where it flowers profusely and also makes a splendid wind-break, corners being among the draughtiest spots in the garden. In climates warmer than ours it can be classed as a winter-flowerer, being out frequently in February and even January. On our exposed hill-top it usually starts in early April; only once has it flowered in March—on the 31st. One cold spring it was as late as 24 April. It grows in any soil, stands up to all winds and weather and is said to thrive even in a sunless and smoky town atmosphere. A shrub of many virtues!

In bloom about the same time is *V carlesii*, a deciduous Korean shrub, again wonderfully fragrant and with flower-heads very similar to those of *V burkwoodii*, of which it is one parent. Another nicely rounded bush, though not so tall and certainly less tough, it appreciates some shelter from rough winter weather. We have it between a wall—on the north-east side—and a massive bush of the evergreen *Osmarea burkwoodii* to the south-west. The osmarea gets the full force of the gales and never turns a hair; the viburnum thrives in its shelter.

Easily the most spectacular viburnum at all times of the year is the Chinese evergreen *V rhytidophyllum*, which has leaves up to 10in long and may grow as high as 20ft. Clearly it is not a shrub for the small garden, being rather like one of the vaster rhododendrons in its proportions. The huge leaves are most conspicuous, long and fairly pointed, grey-green and deeply wrinkled all over the upper side and thickly grey-felted below. White flowers in May and June are followed by berries which change from red to a shiny black.

At the other end of the scale is the low spreading *V davidii*, also from China. About 2ft high, it is a most useful compact evergreen for the front of a border. The large oval leathery leaves are a bright dark green, tapering at the base to short dark-red stems, and conspicuously marked with three long parallel veins so that they have an almost folded look. If you have both male and female plants the clusters of flowers in late April or early May will be followed on the female bush by beautiful bright blue berries.

For winter flowering it is difficult to beat the popular laurustinus, *V tinus*. When one sees it over every other garden wall one is apt to feel a little snobbish about it, which is foolish, for no shrub is more floriferous—a quality not to be despised in winter. It makes a dense evergreen bush, up to 10ft high and more across; and it is clothed to the ground from November to April with a continuous show of clustered heads of white flowers and pink buds.

Much more delicate in appearance is the deciduous *V fragrans*, which forms a rather narrow, upright bush. One spray of the pink-tinged white flowers will scent a whole room, and they may appear at any time between September and March, depending on the weather. Although Farrer found it growing wild in high bleak places in the mountains of China, in this country it repays a little shelter. A near relative is the handsome *V grandiflorum*, which closely resembles it, although the flowers are larger and the growth stouter. Best of all, perhaps, is the hybrid of these two, *V bodnantense*, which seems to be more vigorous in some gardens (see picture on page 20). Both *V grandiflorum* and the hybrid do better than *V fragrans* in mine, but I suspect that may be because it is growing in a more exposed position.

One final virtue of nearly all these viburnums is that they provide attractive cut flowers for the house. In a flat bowl their rounded heads of white or pink-tinted flowers look delightful, usually smell delicious and can be arranged in a trice. Cutting for the flower vase means, in effect, pruning the shrub, so that some care is needed, particularly with the winter-flowering ones. But from shrubs as floriferous as the spring-flowering viburnums it is usually quite easy to pick all you want without harm.

MOSCHATEL

Good mortal, do not mock,
Come prove our pledge:
The faeries' Town Hall Clock
Stands in this hedge.
As sure as Sprinkling Tarn
Lies high and cold,
As sure as whin is gold,
Here you may learn

How, wondrously designed,
One tiny flower
Signals to every wind
The April hour;
As sure as honey-bee
Thrives in the sun,
As sure as wagtails run,
Here you may see
(If you but look aright
While I count ten)
BIG BEN
The very height
For Jenny Wren.

Anne Johnson

FLOWER TIMEKEEPERS W.E.D.

Linnaeus's idea was to plant a clump of flowers known to open at
3am, then a clump which opened at 4am, and so on. These natural
clocks could of course give only approximate times, and the times
of opening and closing applied only to fine, sunny days; in cloudy,
misty, or rainy weather flowers remain closed, or only partly open,
irrespective of the time.

The duration of a plant's 'sleep' varies from ten to twenty hours,
the average being rather more than fourteen. Sometimes a blossom
will open and close for as many as twelve days in succession; others
will open once or twice only and then wither.

Linnaeus made use of many wild flowers for his clock. As it was
constructed at Upsala, and the opening and shutting of plants
varies in different latitudes, his clock could not be copied exactly
in England. But here are facts about flowers which could be used
in our latitudes. Wild roses open between 4am and 5am. Many
species of flax between 5am and 6am. Willow herb between 6am
and 7am. Many gentians, speedwells and wood-sorrels between
8am and 9am. Most tulips and opuntias between 9am and 10am.
Centaury and chaffweed between 10am and 11am. Potentilla

between 11am and noon. No plant in our latitude opens during the afternoon, but several close, such as hawkweed, mesembryanthemum, calendula, alyssum, flax. Evening primrose and campion open at 6pm. Between 7pm and 8pm Dame's violet and catchflies open. Woodruff and tobacco between 8pm and 9pm. And from 9pm to 10pm, expect the cactus.

There are even a few flowers, such as one of the gentians, meadow saffron, and flax, which will go on opening and closing when the weather is cloudy with bright intervals.

THE STRANGE STORY OF THE AURICULA
Professor Sir Rowland Biffen, FRS

Attempts to trace the history and origin of our old-fashioned garden plants form one of the many pleasant byways of horticulture. It is a task which can keep one busy throughout the year, for it involves a study of the literature of bygone centuries during the dead season, and the more practical work of cultivating every variety one can raise or acquire during the growing period.

I drifted by slow stages into a study of the auricula. 'Study' is perhaps a too high-sounding word to use for what came to be in reality a mere pottering with complex scientific problems which are to be solved with any approach to finality only by someone with the resources of a considerable research station at his disposal. However, the incompleteness of the following account of its results may be a meritorious feature, for it may lead some other gardener to carry the story still further.

The cultivation of the auricula has a long and, in some respects, well-documented history. It dates back in this country to at least 1597, when the first description of the plant was published in Gerard's classic *Herball*. By then it was apparently widely grown on the continent, and the tradition that it was introduced here by refugees from the Netherlands about the year 1575 may well be based on fact. It became an established garden plant rapidly, for in Sir Thomas Hanmer's *Garden Book*, printed in 1659, some forty named varieties are described.

Even at this early period the colour range was a wide one, for he mentions 'yellow, white, haire colour, oronge, cherry, crimson, purple, violet, murrey, tawny, olive, cinnamon, ash, dun,' and others. Other contemporary accounts add still further to this list. These descriptions can convey only a vague impression of the flowers of the seventeenth century, but fortunately the Dutch and Flemish artists of the period included many auriculas in the noble bunches of flowers they delighted in painting. These show that the old-world varieties were counterparts of those now grown in our borders under the name of alpine auriculas, except that the present-day varieties are decidedly more rich and vivid in colour. But, though the soft dove-grey, *café-au-lait* browns and quiet purple tints are no longer to be found among the plants raised from commercial seed, they occur still in many of the plants in cottagers' gardens.

In addition to this long series of coloured forms, two distinct types—the double and the striped auricula—had come into existence. The double, once a highly appreciated flower, is no longer obtainable in commerce, but a few of its once numerous varieties still find a place in amateurs' collections. They lack so many of the characteristics of the present-day flowers, however, that few florists now have any interest in them. Further, if those I have grown are at all representative, they have the distressing habit of throwing trusses of single flowers as often as double. The striped forms, which, in their day, were outstandingly popular and often extraordinarily expensive, have become scarcer still. In fact they are said to be extinct. But I have been fortunate enough to raise a few, and hope they may prove a nucleus for the recovery of the race, for their gay colour-effects are a pleasing foil to the quiet formality of the show auriculas.

It was only after some three centuries of cultivation that the origin of these alpine auriculas was discovered. Then Kerner's observations made it practically certain that the plants first collected in the high Alps were natural hybrids between two very unlike species, *Primula hirsuta* and *P auricula*. The former has rosy-pink flowers and bright green foliage, the latter sweetly scented yellow flowers and, for the most part, leaves with a silvery cast. This effect arises from the green ground of the leaf being obscured to a variable extent by a coating of microscopic glandular hairs—the 'meal' of the florists. If slight, the leaf colour is a grey-green; if dense, white. It may also be concentrated on edges of the leaves, thus outlining them with an exquisite silver margin. Kerner's views, much criticised at the time and then more or less forgotten, are undoubtedly correct, though the full story is more complex than could be forseen in the days when plant breeding was a mystery rather than a somewhat bewildering science.

During the period 1650–1750 no changes are recorded in the make-up of the flower, and an observer might well have considered that it was more or less stabilised, and that further striking changes were unlikely. But about the end of the period there occurred one of the most extraordinary developments known to florists, when a strange and totally distinct type of auricula came into existence. This had two outstanding characteristics: the edges of the flowers were green, grey or white, and in the centre of each was a zone of shining white meal—the 'paste'—a feature still unknown in any other flower. This sudden change (for no one can imagine that any-one thought of a flower with these characteristics and then set out to build it up by a process of selection) was the result of the replace-ment of the normal petals by structures which, even in microscopic details, are identical with the foliage leaves. The paste, too, is a leaf characteristic seen to perfection at the base of the leaves form-ing the calyx of the flower. The green, grey and white edges of the flowers thus represent the various stages of mealiness seen in the foliage of *P auricula*.

The mutation started the auricula off on a new course of develop-ment. The presence of the paste, which added immensely to the attractiveness of this strange flower, had one disadvantage, for, solid as it appears to be, a single drop of rain ruins it. This led to the auricula becoming a pot plant and hence, almost inevitably, an exhibition plant. So rapidly did this phase of its culture extend that by 1798, in the interests of judges and exhibitors alike, florists found it necessary to determine the 'points' of flowers suitable for the show-bench, and a schedule of seventeen requirements was drawn up which, almost unchanged, still defines the perfect flower.

By the beginning of the nineteenth century the edged auricula had become everyone's flower, and surviving nurserymen's catalogues show that hundreds of distinct varieties had been raised. Coloured plates of a large selection of these were published in 1828 in Sweet's 'Florist's Guide' and show that the flower, by then, had reached a stage of perfection equal to that of the present day.

These early years of the nineteenth century form a peculiarly interesting horticultural period. Gardeners were no longer content with the natural beauty of their flowers, and they sought a formality and refinement which, once seen, is immediately appreciated, although it is difficult to describe. It is dependent on the combination of a complex of attributes such as the proportions of the various parts of the flower, the shape of its outline, its markings, its texture, and so on. The assembly of all these features constituted as difficult a breeding problem as one could ask for, and even nowadays it has to be admitted that the resulting production of the perfect flower is mostly a matter of chance. Still, it was tackled, and by none more thoroughly than the weavers and miners of Lancashire, who during the 1850s were producing flowers which, hearsay has it, were the finest ever raised.

There is nothing known so far as to the date when the two other sections into which auriculas are classified put in their first appearance. One of these, the 'fancy,' is in reality an edged auricula in which the colour brought in by *Primula hirsuta* has disappeared, leaving the flower a symphony in green and golden-yellow. Good and distinctive varieties are easily raised, but the group has never been so popular as the second, known as the 'selfs'. The sumptuous colouring of these selfs and the presence of a paste suggest that they are hybrids between alpine and edged varieties, and crosses between these sections tend to confirm this view. But they do appear in families raised from self-fertilised seeds from both the grey- and white-edged plants, so that a multiple origin seems almost a certainty, and only further breeding experiments can clear the matter up. They are well worth the making, for the mixture of plants which result will almost certainly contain a few fit to be included in any amateur's collection.

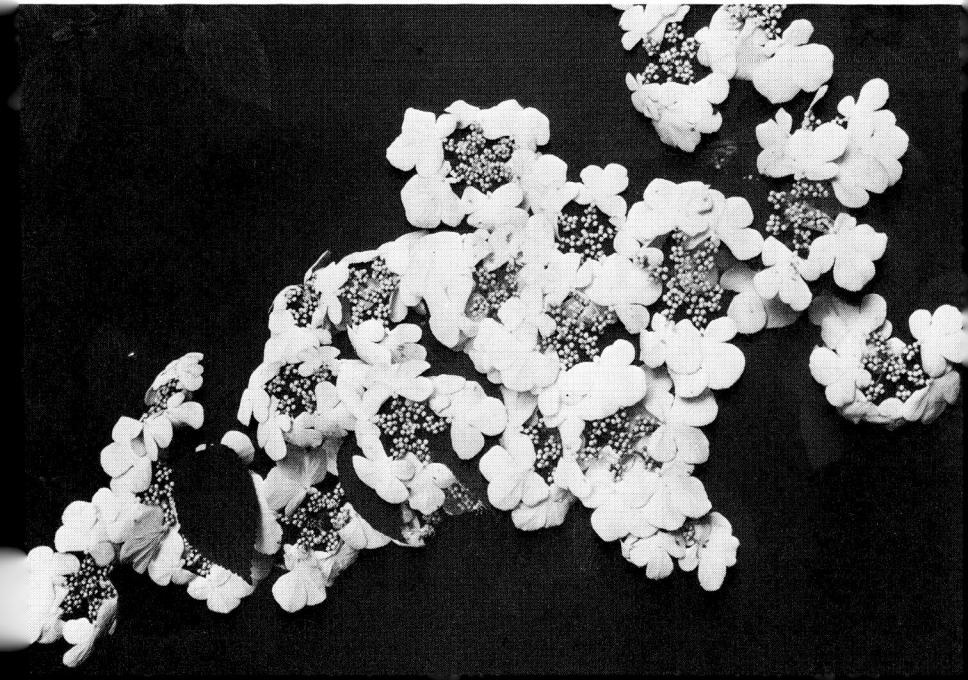

THE MODERN IRIS   John Street

Irises, of one sort or another, can be had in flower all the year round and, with a little imagination, in any colour you care to choose. All this follows from a world-wide range of species and an astronomical number of hybrids. The first to flower is that old favourite of the modern outdoor winter garden *Iris stylosa*, as it is still known, though its correct name is hiccough—*unguicularis*. It often starts to flower in November, and grows best in bad soil and a draughty position. But it will be later in a mild winter, because it needs the stimulus of frost to bring it into flower.

Green-flowered Iris from Afghanistan

The small gap in the iris display which existed in the late spring is being filled to overflowing by a new range of hybrids called the 'medians'. They have mostly been raised by crossing the tall bearded irises, which are sometimes too tall for small gardens, with the best forms of the dwarf species *pumila*, which are found in Austria. Some of these halfway plants—they grow from 6in to 12in—were raised as a sideline by G. A. Darby of Welwyn, who is famous as a breeder of lilies. Three of his are Austrian Sky, blue like the name; Bright Eyes, Lemon Yellow; and Charming Morn, white with a touch of blue.

Tastes change in flowers as much as in anything else; Constance Spry showed how soft colours in quiet tones could be as exciting as the brightest chrysanthemum that ever bounced out of a florist's shop. Another new race of iris hybrids is the *regelio-cyclus* group of crosses between a species from Israel and one from Turkestan. They make excellent cut flowers, lasting long in water and with a rare colouring of fine stripes on a quiet background. One of the latest of these is Sylphides, whose big grey petals are flecked with brown and emphasised by a darker spot at the base.

Late irises for July were at one time limited to the varieties of the 'clematis-flowered iris of Japan,' *Iris kaempferi*—and very lovely they are too. They have immense wide-open flowers, in purple and white, sometimes as much as 12in across. But they must have an acid soil, like rhododendrons and azaleas. Now some July-flowering plants which will be less fussy about soil are being developed from the wild irises of Louisiana. These have been saved from destruction by enthusiasts in the Deep South who rescue the wild plants from the swamps before they are drained, bulldozed and built over.

New forms are still being found in other parts of the world. In the winter of 1964–5 Admiral Paul Furse found a new green-flowered species in Afghanistan. It was a solitary plant which had survived the passage of a tribe through a valley. Normally, they leave nothing; everything green is eaten to the ground. But this one iris species, orchid-like in form, was growing a little higher up out of the way of the animals.

There are exciting developments in the popular tall bearded varieties. All over the world new hybrids are being raised with bigger flowers in better shapes and all sorts of colours. True pink is still elusive, but it may come from two directions at once. It will either be a mauve that has been purged of the purple undertone, like Lavanesque, an 'orchid' pink, or Benton Cordelia; or it will be one of the buff-apricots with more emphasis on the salmon shading, less orange and yellow. Party Dress, with ruffled petals in flamingo pink (a catalogue euphemism for apricot) is about the best of these and a lovely flower by any standard; yet it is still not true pink, except through the rose-coloured spectacles of the enthusiast.

Frills are new to the iris, and they were one of the attractions of the British raised Dancer's Veil (white edged with blue), which won all possible prizes all over the world in 1964. But the flowers of all are generally larger and better displayed. White flowers are not universally popular, but the iris is the exception: one of the most widely planted is Cliffs of Dover, which was raised in America. At the other extreme are the very dark colours: mahogany, rich purple and deep orange. Blue-eyed Brunette is a rare mixture of colours—cigar brown, deep rich purple, a tiny spot of bright blue and an orange beard. Here is a selection in the modest price range to make the old blues in the patch by the back door look even more forlorn: Dotted Swiss, blue and white, frilled; Lady Louise, yellow and cream; Benton Cordelia, mauve that is close to pink; Christobel, a copper-red; and the White Cliffs of Dover. The time to plant is from June to October in any soil that is dry. Irises like lime but, surprisingly, some of the experts are getting excellent results by digging in peat before planting.

ROSES BY THE SEA   Margaret Stanley-Wrench

When we first came to our seaside home, the garden was a lawn of tussocky, salty grass, bordered by dry banks. One old and straggling rose climbed and lost itself in a hedge. The soil, however, turned out to be clay, and there was protection from thick walls of cupressus, escallonia and euonymous, and plenty of sun; so we said, 'Roses', and a selection of what were then modern varieties, as well as the classic old ones, like York and Lancaster, Rosa Mundi and R centifolia, were soon in what seemed an ideal habitat. But shocks were in store. First, there was the wind. In our village we are lulled for days by pellucid air, cloudless blue skies and a sea that purrs on the sand. Then, in a matter of moments, the south-west wind will leap out at you, and every plant is flattened, every unsheltered leaf blackened with salty spray. Our roses, in their south-facing borders, lost most of their buds, and the rest were eaten by hordes of caterpillars which had slumbered in the escallonia. The cupressus hedge sucked up all the water—and manures —and flourished; not so the roses.

Plenty of trials and innumerable errors have finally taught us which roses to grow and how to place them. The sturdy Edwardian and Georgian veterans are best for general purposes—Madame Butterfly and Madame Abel Chatenay; General MacArthur, which likes our mild climate and will bloom from June to January, giving us excellent, fully scented roses at Christmas; Caroline Testout, because it reminds us of strawberry ices and garden parties; George and Hugh Dickson, for their scent and prolific blooming; and Frau Karl Druschki, snow in midsummer. Oddly, the more modern roses do not do so well with us, except the Poulsens, which accompany General MacArthur on its winter-blooming exploits.

We allow our more vigorous bush roses to grow tall, keeping them at the back of sheltered beds, with polyantha types or Scotch briars towards the front. These briars are among the best seaside roses; in its wild state *R spinosissima* grows half buried in sand, on windy cliffs of the slopes of bleak, chalky downs. The double yellow and double white make charming edges for rose beds or can be grown as a low hedge. Stanwell Perpetual, the shell-pink hybrid, makes a larger bush and blends well with hybrid polyanthas.

As large bushes, which seem to enjoy salt air, the *Rosa* species are excellent. *R moyesii* reaches to 8ft and bears flat, terra-cotta flowers of wonderful texture, like wax and taffeta blended. In autumn the fruits resemble long flaming urns, and the ash-shaped leaflets are very graceful. *R cantabridgensis*, another hybrid, has lemon-yellow flowers in May and early June, and fronded leaves of a fresh and delicate green. Other favourites are *R rubrifolia*, with wood and leaves of deep plum colour, bloomed with blue-green, and glowing hips in autumn; and *R mirifica*, with leaves and thorns just like those of gooseberries, invaluable for misleading friends, for what appears to be a gooseberry bush is covered in large, single rose-pink blooms. The hips are like spiky gooseberries, too. Another trap for friends is *R viridiflora*, which has greenish-brown flowers, more like sea-anemones than roses.

All these *Rosa* species are best suited to wilder and less formal parts of a garden, and here, too, the Rugosas will fit in, for they like plenty of room and, if allowed, will send up suckers and cover yards of ground with their thick, jade-green, quilted leaves and scented flowers. Blanc Double de Coubert is a lovely clear white, Pink Grootendorst has flowers like tiny fringed pinks, and Parfum de l'Hay smells like the otto of roses of your dreams. The single varieties yield hips as large as gooseberries, which make excellent jams and jellies.

Moss roses also enjoy sea air. Common Pink Moss, a sentimental, chintz kind, makes a good climber if trained up a trellis. As a Mr Wrench, nurseryman at Fulham, first raised the white moss rose in England, we feel we must include Blanche Moreau, best of the double whites, in our collection, and also Gloire des Mousseuses, which is like an old flower painting, with large, rose-pink, heavily mossed blooms.

Mildew flourishes in the mild seaside climate, in spite of sulphur, so we find it unwise to grow roses against the house, except American Pillar—dull but possessing salt-resistant, glossy foliage. Albéric Barbier smothers fences with evergreen leaves and flowers like finest whipped cream. This rose blooms nearly all the year round with us and resists gales and frost. So do Excelsa and Dorothy Perkins, which bloom up to Christmas. Blaze, Allan Chandler and Paul's Scarlet Climber flourish as pillar roses, while, on an east-facing wall, Etoile de Hollande has flowered in time for Easter.

For their place in history and romance, we have York and Lancaster, which makes a fine specimen bush of 5ft to 6ft with hundreds of blush, cerise and white flowers, and Rosa Mundi, almost a dwarf, with flat, striped flowers, deep rose on palest blush, with staring yellow 'eyes,' and very sweet scent. It is best grown on the edge of a sunny bed and can make a charming edging rose, as can dwarf Chinas, smaller still. But the rose which I would not be without, the queen of them all, is Zephyrine Drouhin—thornless, incomparable of scent, hardy, lovely in bud and bloom, and so prolific and long in its blooming season. It can be grown as a large specimen bush or as the scrambling type of climber; if it is pegged down, it will cover the bed with its rosy blossoms.

Hand-picking and early spraying with nicotine have controlled the caterpillars. Experience has shown us where the winds cut, and there we plant downy-leaved, wind-resisting varieties or use hurdles as wind-breaks. A mulch of grass cuttings and sprayings of liver of sulphur and soft soap keep down mildew and black spot, and nightly rinsings of sun-warmed water help to keep leaves free of salt and wash away aphis and mildew spores.

So, in our seaside garden we have the best of both worlds—modern and old together; Crimson Glory and old MacArthur; Pink Moss and The Doctor; R moyesii and Betty Uprichard—history in a flower bed. For after all, the history of the rose goes side by side with that of mankind, and Rosa Mundi, mistress of a medieval king, and York and Lancaster, memorial of a nation's discord, blend easily and peacefully with royalty, general or celebrity of today.

SHAW'S PIPPIN   N. W. Barritt

In June, 1931, G.B.S. complained, in a letter to his district council, of the nuisance caused in Ayot St Lawrence and its neighbourhood by a refuse dump at Wheathampstead. 'In March,' he wrote, 'I was cruising the Mediterranean, where I was very strongly reminded of the dump by the fumes of the island volcano of Stromboli, which is believed by the islanders to communicate directly with hell, and to be, in fact, one of the chimneys of that establishment. I was able to assure them that this could not be the case, as our Wheathampstead volcano, which has no crater, is a much greater nuisance.' On his return he found the dump 'in full blast,' but a much more danger-ous nuisance than the smell had developed. 'To explain its gravity is beyond my literary powers: therefore, I will ask the District Council to allow me to quote the Eighth Chapter of the Book of Exodus, verses 21–4: "Behold I will send swarms of flies upon thee".' Shaw had already had cause in previous years to complain about the nuisance. 'What happens every four years is, evidently, that the covering up is allowed to fall behind the dumpings; and the uncovered refuse catches fire and Strombolizes us, while the un-burnt stuff breeds billions of flies.'

The letter was forwarded to the Islington Borough Council, who owned the dump, and, after an inspection, they denied the nuisance. In reply, Shaw pointed out that his first letter was not written in the interests of 'merry Islington,' so that 'the perfect satisfaction of its Cleansing Superintendent and Medical Officer is no satisfaction to me'. He went on: 'The Wheathampstead dump is twenty miles north of Islington; and at that distance its fragrance is lost. It is about a mile south of my house; and when the wind is in that quarter I am not reminded of Shakespeare's "Sweet south that breathes upon a bank of violets"; I am reminded of Stromboli, of Etna, of Vesuvius and of hell. My famous neighbour, Mr Cherry-Garrard, sole survivor of "the worst journey in the world", after the horrors of which one would suppose that no discomfort possible in these latitudes could seem to him worth mentioning, has written a letter implying plainly that there is little to choose between midwinter at the South Pole and midsummer at Lamer Park when the dump is in eruption.'

In May 1932, when I was employed at Rothamsted on problems

21st Oct. 1936.

I left the monster on exhibition on the drawingroom mantelpiece; but the cook took it and stewed it; and I swallowed some of it before I was told what it was.

I shall never be the same man again; But Mrs Shaw rather liked it

G. Bernard Shaw

of water pollution, I visited the dump out of curiosity and found it inoffensive, but I was impressed by the wealth of blossom on a young apple tree about 6ft in height growing out of the rubbish. When I went to see the tree again in August to examine the fruit, I was disappointed to find only a few deformed specimens, the tree having been considerably damaged. But I was still curious as to the possible merits of such a potentially fruitful tree, so I grafted cuttings on Type IX rootstocks the following spring.

Three years later the tree bore a single apple, which weighed 24oz. When I sent this to G.B.S. it brought in reply the characteristic postcard here reproduced. Although Mrs Shaw's appreciation was from the culinary point of view only, it has since proved to be a worthy dessert apple. After the war I planted up to two acres with it, and now that the trees are coming into bearing, I find that the fruit has a ready sale in competition with well-established varieties.

THE PEAR TREE

In May the pear-tree branches
Blossom and bend low
Under their avalanches
And drifts of snow;

And instantly I remember
How, in the star-blue light
Of snow in late December,
They blossomed in the night.

Clive Sansom

A GARDEN OF OLD-WORLD DIANTHUS

W. L. Carter

William the Conqueror was, I may as well explain, responsible for the beginning of my garden of old pinks and carnations. Around his castle at Falaise grows the wild carnation, *Dianthus caryophyllus*, and a few plants of this laid the foundation of my fragrant, old-world groups. Over the low stone wall at the rear of the pinks hang tangled old bushes of the Scotch rose, in differing colours, with an occasional *R arvensis*. On a sunny site the pinks have flourished for the past eight or ten years. One of the earliest pinks I obtained was Anne Boleyn. This I found in a Herefordshire cottage garden. Anne is a magnificent double blush-coloured pink with a spicy full-bodied fragrance.

It would be interesting to know precisely which Dianthus was used during the Middle Ages for 'Sops in Wine'. 'July-flower' petals were dropped into wine for flavouring before serving. There is an old apple known as 'Sops in Wine' with red streaks running through the flesh, but I have not discerned any carnation flavour or aroma.

One of the oldest of garden pinks is the Old Fringed. This, I find useful for edging, as it forms compact cushions and hummocks bearing numerous small but sweetly perfumed white flowers. Jane Austen, an old single pink, with fringed edges, of a curious mulberry-red, tipped with white, is rampant with me. When I look upon this pleasant little flower I think of the 'Clove July-flowers or Gilly-flowers' of the fifteenth and sixteenth centuries. Bullein in his *Bulwarke of Defence* considered that 'carnations do not only preserve the bodies of men but doth also kepe the minde and spirituall partes from terable and fearful dreames through their heavenly savour and moste sweete pleasant odour', and who shall prove him wrong?

Recently I came across one known as Sutton Pink, derived from Sutton-on-Sea, Lincs, where it was found in a cottage garden. The strong foliage is dark green and its rose-pink blooms are carried on a stiff, erect stem. Donnizetti, another old favourite, came gratis from an old Cornish garden. I had purchased some *Lilium Chalcedonicum* and this was put in with the bulbs marked, 'Name unknown, but good', and it certainly is good. I have it among some rocks. It is rather a dwarf grower—with me, never more than a foot in height. The rich crimson flowers, very freely produced, have a dark zone of ringing in the centre, with the usual delightful aromatic perfume. It seems likely to succeed in wall gardens, for two plants I put in a crevice on a dry wall have done well. Near this one I have Spark, a curious and tiny plant. The foliage looks much like grass with red markings, and this diminutive subject has not yet exceeded a height of three inches. The little flowers which almost hide the plant, so freely are they produced, are of a blood-red colour with an alive look about them. This I had sent me in error for another variety.

Everybody knows, of course, Mrs Sinkins. It breaks every rule of a well-formed bloom. It is a calyx-burster; a ragged, shapeless flower, but its glorious fragrance and old pleasaunce air will keep it in our gardens. The pink sport, although modern, finds a home with its progenitor and these two large drifts are not the least of my pink garden's attractions. From an estate bailiff, who had a garden full of good old things, came Ella, a white and crimson pink; F Millard, a compact plant of short growth with large, double, dull crimson flowers, and Ruth Fischer of like habit with its beautifully shaped heavy double white blooms. With these were sent some of the fine old laced pinks which I have not yet been able to identify. These laced varieties with their purple, red, black and white and what the old-time gardener called rose-leaf lacings are rather slow to increase—they look as if they had ventured forth from the days of the minuet and flowered satins—but the care they demand is cheerfully given.

Of old picotees and carnations there are many in my garden. Most are too similar in colouring although the old country fanciers doubtless had their distinctions. One would like to meet with some of that small collection grown by Sir Thomas Hanmer at his Bettisfield seat about 1670, 'Ish. and 18d. the roote'. He was not very successful with some of his gilliflowers, for he says of one purchase of ten varieties, 'they all died the second year except Dutches of Brabant, Andronicus, Royall Soveraigne, and Adolphus'. All these were of crimson, scarlet or purple and white. Possibly they were put into an unsuitable position as they were 'set in the full earth in the pheasant garden'. John Parkinson (1629) and Gervase Markham (1613) cannot say too much in praise of the carnation. Best of all are the words used by Barnabe Googe (1577), 'Oh what sweete and goodly Gely flowres are here: You may truely say, that Solomon in all his princely pompe was never able to attayne to this beautie'.

The Old Crimson Clove I grow in quantity, because I believe it to be one of the earliest of all carnations, possible even the 'Sops in Wine' or Clove Gilliflower to which reference has been made. True, it bursts its calyx most times. Has it always been a ragged bloom, I wonder. An old book I have, the *Compleat Florist* (1747), shows what may be a nice spray of this carnation but the calyx portrayed is perfect. Perhaps the Old Crimson has fallen into bad habits!

In a separate part of my garden grows a small group of mule pinks. They are supposed to have been produced from crossings of the Sweet William with garden pinks which are hybrids of *Dianthus plumarius*. The stems, foliage and cluster-flowering habit of the plants resemble the Sweet William, but the individual blooms are like small pinks of refined shape. They set no seed and can be propagated only by cuttings or layering. With the exception of the old dwarf, double crimson Sweet William, they are the rarest of all the old pinks and their allies. Gerarde (1597) remarks that 'these Plants are not used either in meate or medicine but esteemed for their beautie to deck up the garden'. I have about a dozen varieties, only half of which are really old in years. The double Rose, with its lovely rose-coloured flowers, grows away near Napoleon III, which, during July and August, is covered with innumerable double, blazing crimson flowers on stems a foot in length. One I call Salmon is a perfect reproduction of Napoleon in salmon colouring. Enid, a rose-pink and Marie Père, a soft blush-rose, are near an unnamed variety which bears many blood-red single flowers. Some little time back I had given me by a disabled war veteran two newer varieties which came from stock he had bought, but he did not say from whom. He told me their names attracted him. They were called Messines Pink, a very delicate shade of salmon-pink, and Messines White, a pure white in colour, this latter being a sport from the pink one. With me they reach a foot high, but I am inclined to agree with my disabled friend that there is some Border carnation blood in them, as the flowers of the cluster have such regular shape. However, they are a welcome addition, and near to them is Emile Parr with its deep salmon-coloured double flowers.

A HEDGEROW SANCTUARY   Jason Hill

The hedgerow between our front garden and the macadam is a sanctuary from plough and builder. It contains three or four hornbeams, oak, holly, blackthorn, hawthorn, dogwood and privet, interlaced with honeysuckle, the ivory white *Rosa arvensis*, and old man's beard. The bank is occupied with woodruff, stitchwort, a small colony of bracken and one of the graceful woodland grasses. We have added to it one or two foxgloves and some wild strawberries, and it has been necessary to remove the old man's beard, for, as a nurseryman's catalogue says very truly, 'it rivals in vigour the lamas of the tropics'; otherwise the hedge has been left, except for careful clipping, in its original state.

It is tempting to recommend the planting of this natural association in a small group, where its good qualities are displayed even better than when it is drawn out into the linear form of a hedge. Stitchwort may be omitted, for its other name (Robin-run-the-Hedge) implies both its agility and the right place for it. Bracken can be a plague in sandy soils, but the delicate fawn of its winter colouring (shared by the stoat and the fallow deer) is singularly beautiful.

With the addition of the common maple, *Acer campestre*, for its autumn colour, this group makes a small and inexpensive wild garden more satisfying and in character than the horde of garden plants run wild, into which this kind of gardening has commonly degenerated.

ORCHID GROWING AS A HOBBY   D. F. Sander

The very word 'orchid' seems to spell 'inhibition' to many a gardener. He considers orchids exotic, and of course most of them are, though no more than the tomato. He imagines them to be expensive and difficult to grow. A few are costly, and a number difficult; but the vast majority are quite easily grown. For those who have reached the age of discretion in gardening, coupled with a loss of vigour where outdoor tasks are concerned, orchids in a greenhouse offer an enormous horizon. When you are tired after the week's work, or maybe if you are a surgeon or musician who cannot afford to harden your hands with the rougher tasks, you will find orchid growing an ideal hobby.

Whereas most plants are pretty perishable, an orchid may resemble a tree in that, once established, it may last for at least a hundred years. On my nursery I have several which date back to the last century, at least one to 1852.

'If only he'd spend half as much time on the garden as he spends on those orchids . . .'

Most amateurs have modest collections in small greenhouses, perhaps only 8ft by 10ft or 10ft by 15ft, where they grow the plants purely for pleasure. An orchid matures slowly, but thereafter flowers once a year. There is a positive challenge in making any plant flower to perfection, but to flower an orchid somehow involves rather more intelligence and thought. True, you can buy books that give good guidance on how to grow them, but in the end you will find yourself discarding most of the advice you have received from various growers. You will give each plant the treatment you find from experience to be best.

Basically orchids are divided into two types: terrestrial and epiphytal. The first do not necessarily grow only in the ground, but also on rocks, debris such as fallen trees and humus-covered banks. Some are truly terrestrial and usually very difficult to grow in Europe in artificial conditions. Among the others which form the vast majority of the terrestrials are such genera as *Cymbidium*, *Phaius* and *Calanthe*, all three popular and free-flowering. They require a compost rich in feeding materials such as a mixture of fibrous loam, peat and bone meal; even well-decayed manure suits calanthes, catasetums and some others. Epiphytes, on the other hand, grow on trees or sometimes on rocks and thrive best in a mixture based on osmunda fibre. In addition to the correct adjustment for acidity, which we effect by the use of sphagnum moss, they require only trace elements present naturally in rain-water. These can also be bought and fed to the plants in liquid form, but I do not advise it except for the advanced amateur grower. Osmunda fibre contains them all in correct proportions.

It is very desirable to have a lesson in potting, the process being difficult to describe. Basically the compost has to be applied in and around the roots so that the homogeneous consistency runs vertically rather than horizontally; this allows water to percolate through the compost to the crocks at the bottom of the pot, drawing air with it from above. In theory orchids are never fed, but in practice cymbidiums and several other terrestrial species are given bone meal or hoof and horn. It is also good practice to spray plants with a leaf feed during the spring and summer months.

Although feeding is contrary to all my instincts, I must concede that some of the most wonderful blooms I have seen during the past ten years have resulted from it. How is it done? A baker's tray or some other convenient shallow container is left on the staging in the greenhouse and filled with water and a few drops of concentrated organic feed. The odd plant which is seen to be wellrooted and growing is left with the base of its pot in the liquid, which it absorbs over the next few hours. The pots may be left in the tray for several days, the resulting slimy growth being washed off later.

When you acquire your first orchids, remember that it is far better to buy a few larger well-established specimens than a quantity of seedlings or of 'direct-import' plants not yet established. These are usually over-advertised from a postal accommodation address and, as no nursery is involved, after-care or advice is not available. Plants that have been grown in open beds and potted up just before sale should be avoided. It is also desirable to have the greatest possible variety within the range the heating capacity of your greenhouse allows.

You will probably start with a 'cool' house: that is, one with a minimum winter temperature of not less than 48° F (10° C), running up in summer to as much as 80° F (27° C), or rather more with sufficient humidity present. Here you would derive great pleasure and satisfaction from a collection of a dozen or so orchids made up on the following lines. ('T' denotes the terrestrials.)

First, three hybrids, and among them one of the many long-lasting *Cymbidium* hybrids (T), preferably large enough to flower within the year; the black bulbs can be readily propagated with bottom heat. The second might be a choice between an *Odontoglossum* and an *Odontioda* hybrid. Either will carry beautiful sprays of flowers, and the second is slightly easier to grow; also its colours are usually heightened by the influence of its red *Cochlioda* parent. For the third hybrid I recommend one of the cypripediums (T), generally known as the slipper orchids. The hybrids are very much larger than the species and are available in flowering sizes.

In addition to the hybrids, all the following species are equally showy and desirable. I start with the green and brown *Cypripedium insigne* (T) and the delicate white and scented *Odontoglossum pulchellum*. *Epidendrum radicans* or *E obrienianum*, both of which carry their orange-to-red flowers in terminal corymbs at the ends of lengthy spikes, will bloom continually for fifteen to eighteen months.

The wonderful button-hole orchid *Dendrobium nobile*, amethyst and white with gold centre, can be left on a shelf, like dahlia tubers, during the winter resting season.

The winter-flowering yellow *Cypripedium insigne sanderae* (T) propagates quickly and is most desirable. I consider *C hirsutissimum* (T) well worth inclusion; the flowers, with a pinkish hue at the tips of the petals, last for six to eight weeks.

No collection would be complete without one or two more dendrobiums. Among these *D densiflorum* has white and gold flowers in pendent thyrsi from the tops of the leafed bulbs, and *D wardianum* has a lovely pink-flushed white flower with heavy yellow markings and slightly scented. The pure white *D jamesianum* remains in flower for three or four months. If I were to throw in one more for luck it would be a lycaste, available in golds, greens and lovely rose colours: say the deep rose *L skinneri* (T).

THE DISCRIMINATING MIMULUS   Richard Morse

If only because of its extraordinary sensitivity, the scarlet mimulus, or monkey-flower, *Mimulus cardinalis*, is worth a place in the garden of anyone interested in the behaviour of plants (see picture on page 71). It is probably one of those species that led Sir Jagadis Bose to the conclusion that 'there is no life-reaction in even the highest animal which has not been foreshadowed in the life of the plant'. The pistil of this mimulus has a two-lobed stigma, the lips of which close when touched. If you dust its lips with its own pollen they will close upon it and remain closed. If you try to deceive them by using grains of sand, or pollen from another species, however, they open again shortly afterwards. They can even discriminate between living and dead pollen from their own species, for if you make them close with dead pollen you will find them wide open a little later.

It is interesting to analyse these selective responses. The closing of the lips is plainly a response to contact with a solid body of any kind. Here there is no discrimination. But whether the lips remain closed or not is a different matter. The reaction here is not mechanical, but chemical. There is, presumably, something in the living pollen of the mimulus that has a numbing action on the plant's movements. The lips, after closing on it, are paralysed by it, and can move no more. The exact nature of the paralysing agent

Page 37 (right) Herbs:
Lavender Cotton, 'Curry
Plant', Lavender, Balm and
Rue; (*below*) Old Rose
Plantain

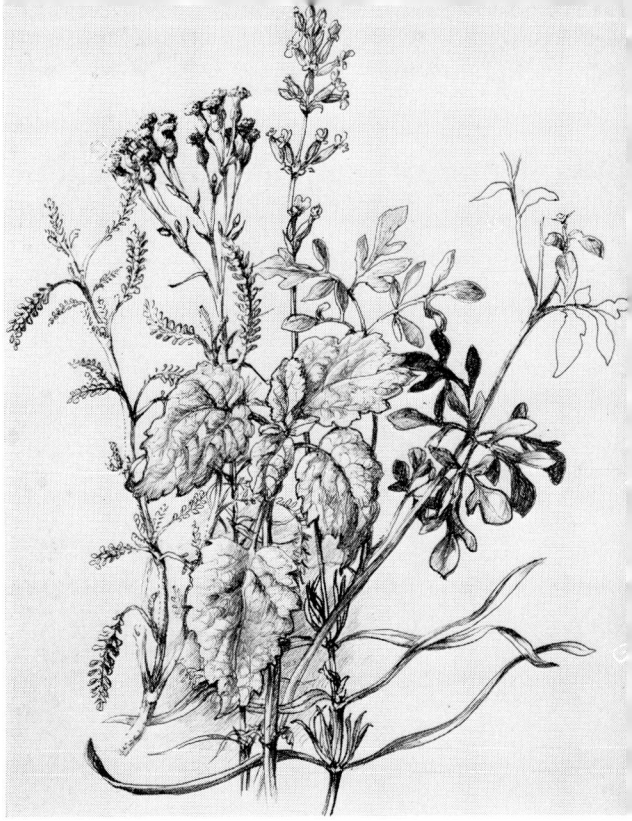

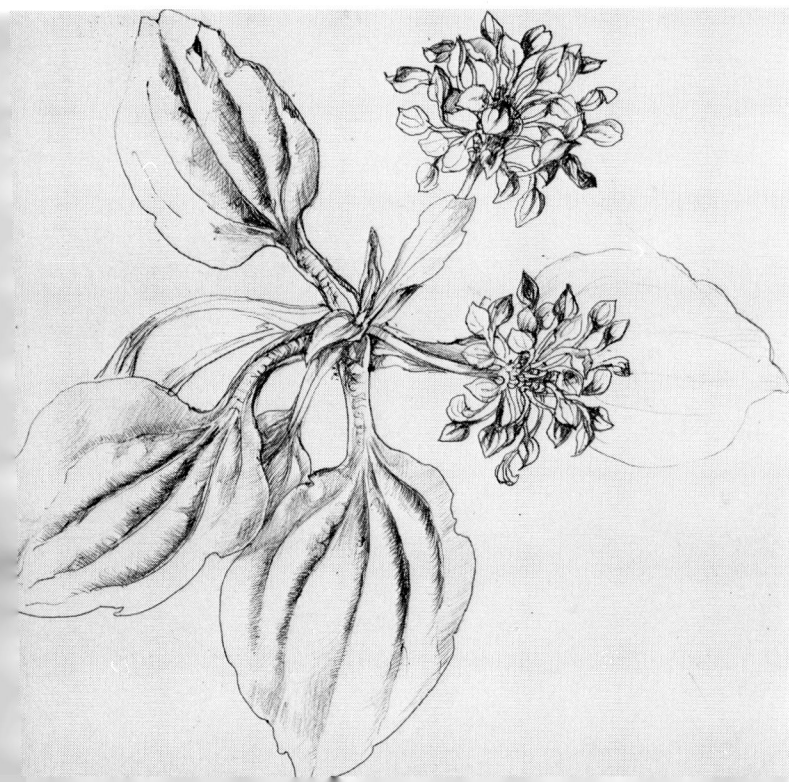

Page 38 (*left*) Hen-and-Chickens
Daisy; (*below*) Double Primroses,
Hose-in-hose and Jack-in-the-Green

does not appear to be known, but there is no doubt about its presence, for when it is extracted and applied to the lips of the stigma, they still close tightly, never to open again. Several other species of mimulus, including the beautiful yellow monkey-flower of our streamsides, show similar responses, and provide fascinating material for experiments.

SECRETIVE DOG ROSES Rona Hurst

Who would guess the secrets hidden behind the fragrant blushes of the common dog-rose? These roses have defied all efforts to give them a normal classification. Hundreds and thousands of species, varieties and forms have been distinguished; each country, each province, each valley has its own peculiar types. But the most curious thing about them is that they are able to set seed without fertilisation. In other words, the offspring are produced by virgin birth and reproduce exactly the mother plant since they have not received any paternal characters.

Microscopical examination shows them to be abnormal in other ways. In each cell of every plant and animal is a specific number of minute bodies known as chromosomes, the bearers of the genes which produce all the reactions which go to build up an individual. Usually a plant reproduces itself by combining half its chromosomes with half the chromosomes of the plant by which it is fertilised, so that the new plant contains a full complement of chromosomes, each parent having contributed half. Hundreds of normal species and varieties of roses behave so. For instance, the musk or field rose of our hedges, *Rosa arvensis*, has 14 chromosomes (seven pairs); the Scotch or Burnet rose, *spinosissima*, has 28, the favourite Chinese species, *R Moyesii*, 42, and the Arctic *acicularis* 56—all multiples of seven. But the dog-roses have 35 chromosomes of which only 14 form pairs, leaving 21 unpaired. They form a few fertile pollen grains which contain only 7 chromosomes but they form egg-cells bearing 28 chromosomes. In this curious fashion a normal fertilisation, in which pollen grains contribute 7 to the 28 chromosomes in the egg-cells, again reproduces the original number, 35; but there is much infertility, and, since they have the power, these plants almost universally reproduce without fertilisation at all. Since many embryo-sacs are produced, it is probable that, side by side with normal, reduced ones, there exist sacs containing the full number of 35 chromosomes, so that, if no fertilisation takes place, seeds and plants can still be produced. This is one of the most amazing adaptations in the plant world, for their curious chromosome behaviour shows that the dog-roses are really ancient hybrids between species with low and high chromosome numbers, which normally should have died out.

The theory is that they arose during the Ice Age, their distribution coinciding approximately with the range of the ice. Today, rose species with seven pairs of chromosomes are all more or less subtropical, while those with higher numbers grow more and more to the north, or higher up mountain ranges, according to the increase of their chromosome number. If this distribution was similar before the Ice Age—we know from fossil remains that roses existed in the Miocene—as the ice spread it would push the high-numbered species down among the low-numbered whose retreat would be prevented by the Mediterranean, Black and Caspian Seas. It may be that the ancient Arctic species, owing to the difficulty of pollen formation in the short northern summers, already had the faculty for non-sexual seed formation. Numerous hybridisations would take place, and, by their power to carry on without any fertilisation, these ancient hybrids managed, not only to survive, but to become the most predominant of all European roses, populating the greater part of Europe and the extreme west of Asia as the ice retreated.

No one doubted that they were perfectly normal species, although puzzling ones, until recent microscopical and genetic experiments revealed their secrets. New forms of the various hybrids would arise by occasional fertilisations or direct mutations, becoming at once fixed since they were simply handed on without being swamped by normal fertilisation. Hence the multitude of species, varieties and forms which confronts the modern botanist, causing him to tear his hair and swear that the dog-roses are beyond working out.

SOW YOUR HARDY PERENNIALS   R. M. Glennie

Many perennials can be grown quite easily from seed, and the young plants require little space; but a good seed bed is essential. It should be sited in the sun, with as much shelter as possible from cold winds. Fork into the top few inches a light dressing of short old compost, or damp horticultural peat laced with superphosphate of lime at the rate of 2oz per sq yd, and leave to settle for a few weeks. Then fork again lightly, tread and rake to obtain a fine tilth. Towards the end of May there is almost sure to be a period when the ground is in the moist warm condition that encourages quick

Planting hardy perennials

germination. Most of the seeds I shall mention are fairly small, so the drills need not be more than half an inch deep. Allow a foot between the rows; and if the seed is sown fairly thinly, the plants can remain in the bed until planting-out time, so avoiding any check during the growing season. If you must sow in dry weather, soak the drills a few hours beforehand or put a light layer of damp peat in the bottom of the drills.

First on my list is coreopsis; but be sure to ask for perennial seed, as there are also annual varieties. Sunburst has cheerful golden-yellow flowers, often 3in across and double, from July to September. Tough stems, 2ft to 3ft high, hold the flowers above strong leafy growth through the worst of our summer weather. The young plants can safely be set out in early autumn and will flower the following summer. Alternatively they can be put in their flowering positions, 15in apart, in March or April.

Next comes *Incarvillea delavayi*; the rose trumpet-shaped flowers on stiff 2ft stems and clump of deeply serrated radical leaves make a striking midsummer plant after two seasons. A native of western China, it should be hardy. Some authorities consider it requires protection in winter, but this has not been my experience in the east of Scotland, 400ft above sea level. The top growth dies back in winter to a large fangy root, so I take the precaution of marking the sites of the plants. Mine are in groups next to daffodils, the fairly large leaves helping to hide the unsightly dying foliage of the bulbs. Do not be alarmed if the plants fail to appear in early spring; they are late starters. In my garden the purplish-green shoots may not show until the end of April, when they make rapid progress.

Another favourite is the globe-flower, *Trollius*, which always does well if plenty of moisture is available. Again the top growth vanishes in winter, fat spear-shaped buds appearing in April. The bright buttercup flowers and large palmate leaves make a welcome splash of colour from late May into June. Varieties range through gold, orange and yellow. I have had a globe-flower in bloom in one year from a May sowing, but a seedling has to do well in its first season to achieve this. No special attention is required after planting beyond a yearly mulch of old compost and a dressing of general fertiliser in early spring.

No perennial border is complete without aquilegias, known north of the Border as granny's mutch. Of the fine strains now available the McKana Giant Hybrids are outstanding. The seed is sometimes slow to germinate, and I have usually to wait two years for a good display. Mounds of pale green foliage appear in early spring, when much of the garden is still asleep. The flowers, on wiry 2ft stems, range from lemon, cream and white to pink, mauve, maroon and purple—in fact through most of the colours of the rainbow.

Scent is another necessary, and what better plant to provide it than lavender? The dwarf Munstead strain is suitable for edging a much frequented path; it also makes compact clumps at the front of a border. The seed germinates easily, and the young plants are ready for their permanent quarters in early autumn. The dwarf strain quickly establishes itself and grows about a foot high.

That almost indestructible plant the perennial evening primrose is worth its place; and *Oenothera missourensis*, a trailer, grows easily from seed. During most of the summer the lemon flowers 3in across, make a fine show against the red stems and calyces. Plant six together, and leave 2ft to 3ft between groups. Good drainage seems to be the only essential for this long-lived plant.

FASHION PARADE

> Damson, then plum, then pear
> For our delight,
> With cherry next, all wear
> Such wondrous white
> That after these
> Breath-taking trees
> Apple could hardly bring
> A thrill, you'd think;
> But apple knows a thing
> And puts on pink.

Cyril Shingler

TAIL CORN

A lady gardener asked the shopkeeper on his doorstep whether his neighbour, outside whose gate the horse had 'obliged,' was likely to want the droppings. 'No, 'e don't want it,' was the reply. 'You take it. Anyway 'twas my friend's 'orse wot done it.'

SUMMER

THE GARDEN

God Knows!

We sow with all the art we know and not a plant appears.
A single seed from any weed a thousand children rears.
If we could weed and seed and sow,
and plant and water, shade and grow
By wishing, dreaming, weeping, willing,
thinking, feeling, speaking, trilling,
And thus the wells and rivers filling,
Would gardens more harmonious blow
Than in the way of soil and stone
Of sun and rain and wind and snow?
'Twould hardly be so good, I trow.

E.K.

THE FLOWER SHOW

Mrs Peters and
Penelope Masters

From Mrs Peters, The Hall, Ditton-Bishop, to her Sister
My Dear, As usual, the flower show was a huge success and
William actually managed to collect six firsts. You'll never guess
who came down for it. Penelope Masters! It was actually her first
real flower show. Naturally she'd been to the Chelsea one, but that
hardly counts, does it?—none of the *fun* there is at ours. I don't
think dear Penelope quite realised the *kind* of clothes to wear. If it
had been a fine day—of course it never is for the flower show—her
suede shoes and lovely Ascot frock would have been *most* appropp-
riate. But it just chanced to be rather wet and I really don't quite
know where Penelope thought one *has* flower shows, but she seemed
a bit upset when she found we had to go right across the vicarage
field to reach the tents. I had my brogues and burberry, and
William was really very good about holding an umbrella over
Penelope. Once we got inside she seemed quite interested in the
peas and beans, and she was really most amusing about the marrows, though I was rather glad the rector could not quite catch
what she said. Of course I'm thoroughly broad-minded myself, and

47

marrows have sometimes struck me as being rather *coarse*. Penelope must have been rather overdoing it with all those night clubs because, just as we were talking about potatoes, she suddenly clutched my arm and said, 'My dear, I'm afraid I'm going to faint!' Of course I offered to go home with her, but she said it was just through being shut up in the tent, and might William drive her home? It meant poor William missing my judging but he was *very* good about it.

Ever
Maud

Penelope Masters to Her Cousin

Sylvia. If ever your life depends on going to a flower show, just die. It's quicker. My dear, can you imagine it? I thought the wretched affair was in the *town hall*! I did wonder why Maud wound herself up in her old burberry, but you know what she is. Of course it was raining, but I thought that going by car and being indoors it would rather cheer up the squires and people to see some clothes that weren't home-grown. Well, we'd only gone a little way when the car stopped. Maud shouted in that dreadful *hearty* way of hers, 'Here we are!' and I found we had to squelch our way over the most enormous field. I nearly lost both my heels and I was smothered in mud and simply soaked. William *thought* he was holding an umbrella over me, but being him it just dripped. At last we got to a floppy tent. My dear, you never smelt such a smell of hot, wet people, mixed up with earth! Crowds of women in tweeds with faces like horses and not a lick of paint among them—just as God and the weather made them! Why do they call it a flower show? There were little piles of vegetables and the most obscene-looking marrows. Well, my dear, we counted every pea and measured every bean, and Maud told me some tale about Pike having no business to have won first prize for cottage potatoes because he grew them in his master's bed. As if I'd have cared if he'd grown them in his pyjamas! Anyhow William seemed to have won every other prize and no one could call the Hall a cottage. When Maud started talking about another tent it finished me. I looked all googly-eyed and said I thought I was going to faint. William drove me home. When we got there we sat by the library fire, and he didn't seem at all in a hurry to get back! Really, my dear, the woman's an imbecile! *Quelle vie!*

Yours, Penelope

OLD-TIME FAVOURITES   Mary McMurtrie

Old-fashioned flowers and gardens, cottage gardens crammed with flowers and great gardens with peaceful lawns, long borders and flowery arbours, all had one thing in common—scent. Gardens were full of scented plants: roses of colours less dazzling than today's but in scent unsurpassed; pinks filling the air with their clove scent on sunny summer days; dusty millers whose fragrance was one of the joys of spring. Mignonette and the evening-scented stock were unobtrusive; you had to look around to discover the source of the scent. Rocket, violet, lily-of-the-valley and many other fragrant flowers were all to be found in old gardens.

Then there were the herbs; they too helped to fill the air with scent. Of the sweet-smelling herbs we nearly all grow lavender and thyme. Among the others were southernwood, sage, mint, marjoram and rosemary; and a great many more were grown and used in days when the housewife was expected to make up her own simple remedies—salves, tonics and teas—as well as home-made wines: costmary, balm, rue, tansy, dill, chamomile, sweet cicely, winter savory, tarragon, caraway and fennel (see pictures on pages 37–38).

I like to have little bags of the dried flowers of lavender among the linen; they give a delightful freshness to sheets and pillow-cases. Sage, thyme, marjoram and mint are useful in the kitchen. The ordinary green mint is best for mint sauce, and the grey furry leaves of the tall apple mint are delicious for flavouring new potatoes and peas. Eau-de-Cologne mint, I have read, was used for making toilet water. Balm can be dried to make a tea which tastes of lemon; the leaves have a spicy aromatic fragrance which made this a favourite stewing herb. The scent of woodruff is strongest when the plant is dried, and it was used for pomanders as well as in bags for linen chests; at the back of the shelves of a closed bookcase it will allay any musty smell. With its whorls of leaves and tiny white flowers this is a pretty little plant for a shady corner of the garden. Caraway seeds were used in seed-cake and buns and also for flavouring cheese; it is a long time since I tasted 'carvie cheese,' though I hear that it is still made.

When I turn to the herbals of Gerard and Parkinson I am always surprised by the variety of plants grown in those far-off days, and especially by the number from abroad: 'out-landish flowers,' Parkinson called them. Nowadays, when we have new and wonderful plants collected from all parts of the world, we forget that about four hundred years ago new and equally wonderful plants and seeds were being brought here from many of the same countries: Persia, Turkey, North Africa, America and the West Indies, as well as from all over Europe. Many of them are still grown, though we may not realise their age. Among the 'out-landish flowers' described by Parkinson in his famous *Paradisi* were daffodils in 'almost an hundred sorts', including the 'Great Yellow Daffodill of Africa' and the 'lesser Barbary Daffodill'; Martagon and other lilies; the Crown Imperial, which came first from Constantinople; tulips in great variety from Armenia, Persia, Turkey, Spain and elsewhere; fritillarias and flower-de-luces (irises); gladioli or 'Cornflagges', colchicums and cyclamen; 'French Cowslips or Beares Eares' (auriculas); the Marvel of Peru; the black hellebore or Christmas flower, and various roses. Besides the exotic plants there were the English garden flowers, among them the 'Carnations and Gilloflowers, the chiefest flowers of account in all our English Gardens'. Also certain roses; 'the White Rose, the Red and the Damaske are the most ancient Standards in England and are therefore accounted naturall'. Then there were violets, rose campions, snapdragons, pansies or 'Hartes Eases', poppies, hollyhocks, 'Sweete Williams and Sweete Johns,' double daisies, peonies, primroses, cowslips and many more.

Carnations and 'gilloflowers' were the favourites of the Elizabethans. Parkinson goes on to call them the 'Queene of delight and of flowers' and describes fifty-two kinds; the 'gilloflowers' were apparently somewhat smaller than carnations but larger than the 'wilde or small Gilloflowers (which wee usually call Pinkes)'. He describes them much more fully than Gerard, who dismisses them briefly, saying that a great volume would not be sufficient, considering that every season brings new sorts. The names and descriptions are delightful: the 'red and gray Hulo'; the White Carnation or Delicate, 'a goodly delightful fair flower in his pride and perfection, that is, when it is both marbled and flaked'; 'the faire maide of Kent, or Ruffling Robin'; 'John Wittie his great tawny Gilloflower'; 'Master Tuggies Princesse' and so on. Pinks were poor relations and came to be appreciated much later; they reached their heyday in the eighteenth and nineteenth centuries, when they were bred to such perfection by the weavers of Paisley and Kilbarchan, whose laced pinks were their special pride. Some have been lost, but it is surprising how many of the old pinks have survived, both the early ones and the laced pinks.

From Elizabethan times double flowers were considered the most desirable, and we read of double periwinkles—we still grow both the blue and the purple—double daisies, and a curious kind which Parkinson called 'double double daisies or childing daisies'; around the double flower is a circle of tiny daisies, and we call it hen-and-chickens. Other old double flowers are bachelors' buttons and fair maids of France, both kinds of double buttercup; double columbines with frilly dumpy flowers known a generation ago as 'granny Mutches'; double violets, marsh marigolds and wallflowers; and a strange plant called the rose plantain, in which the usual spike is shortened into a round leafy 'rose'. It was a 'ferly' and so was welcomed into Elizabethan gardens, and we still have it.

The double primroses, of course, have been quite common for centuries, long lists of the colours being given by various writers. During the last century they were supplanted by the polyanthus, but by the beginning of this one interest in the old double primroses was reviving, new kinds were being evolved and old varieties sought out and restored to gardens. The first double primroses of which we read were the white and the yellow, but the best known today is the double lilac which, I am constantly being told, 'used to grow in my mother's garden long ago'. It was very popular and given such charming names as Quakers' Bonnets, Ladies' Delight and the Evening Primrose. Both Gerard and Parkinson describe and illustrate several other unusual primroses and cowslips: hose-in-hose, in which one flower appears to grow out of another; gallegaskins, which were cowslips with a puffed-out crumpled calyx 'which doe somewhat resemble men's hose that they did weare, and tooke the name of Gallegaskins from thence'. Jack-in-the-Green has its calyx enlarged into five little green leaves which surround the flower like a ruff.

Our native wild roses provided some attractive old garden varieties. The Scots roses were developed from the burnet rose, *R spinosissima*; the thorny bushes covered with little double or semi-double flowers of yellow, pink or white were a familiar sight, especially in cottage gardens, and their scent was entrancing. The sweet briar was hybridised to produce the Penzance briars. The wild white rose, *R arvensis* gave us the Ayrshire roses, of which Dundee Rambler, with large clusters of double white flowers, was perhaps the best known.

The rest of our old roses originated far back through the ages in distant lands.

> *Oh, no man knows*
> *Through what wild centuries*
> *Roves back the rose.*

From China, Persia and eastern Mediterranean lands they came: Damask and Centifolia, Alba, Gallica and, from the East, the musk rose with its wonderful scented cascades of flowers. A rose of ancient origin is the Damask, famous for Attar of Roses, growing in India, Persia and eastern Europe. Most familiar is the York and Lancaster, which bears pale pink, white and parti-coloured blooms on the same bush. Others are the pink Celsiana and Leda, the Painted Damask, very double, its white petals tipped with crimson. The Autumn Damask, *R damascena bifera*, is a rose of great antiquity, believed to have been grown in the gardens of Pompeii. *Rosa alba*, which is among our best known old roses, is hardy and mostly tall; it used to be called the 'tree rose'. Everyone knows the Jacobite rose, *R alba maxima*, Maiden's Blush and the less tall Celestial with blue-green leaves and exquisitely beautiful opening buds of delicate shell-pink. Oldest of all is *Rosa gallica*; it was grown in the twelfth century BC when it was a religious emblem of the Medes and Persians. This semi-double crimson rose, brought home by the Crusaders and still common in old-fashioned gardens, was known as the Apothecary's Rose, as the Red Rose of Lancaster and also as the Rose of Provins. It is a parent of *Rosa mundi*, the best of the 'striped' roses, which is sometimes confused with the York and Lancaster but is quite different; its carmine flowers are striped and flecked with white, though an odd flower may revert to crimson. Another Gallica is Tuscany or the Old Velvet Rose, one of the darkest, whose flat semi-double maroon blooms, lit by bosses of golden stamens, are a wonderful sight when a group is in full flower. The soft rose-pinks and blush and lilac shades of so many of the old roses need the contrast of the darker velvety maroon-crimsons and purples, whose sumptuous depth of colour gives character to a collection. Charles de Mills and Cardinal de Richelieu are two of the darkest, and the curiously named Nuits de Young, which is a little dark maroon moss rose.

In Victorian times the cabbage roses, *R centifolia* and their offspring the moss roses, were great favourites not only in gardens, where cabbage roses hung out voluptuous blooms heavy with their 'hundred leaves' and rich scent, but also in pictures and on embroideries, printed on fabrics and painted on china, and to adorn albums and valentines. Everywhere the conventional round cabbage roses and pink moss rosebuds appeared, often in posies with pansies and other small flowers. The loveliest of the moss roses are the common pink and the white.

Climbing roses covered walls, porches and arbours, and all were scented. The musk rose is among the oldest, and its hybrid the Garland Rose and one of Gertrude Jekell's favourites. Other deliciously scented climbers were the blush Noisette, sometimes called Champney's Pink Cluster, with a clove scent; Félicité et Perpétue; and Céline Forestier, which had a spicy tea scent. Another, more recent (1921) and very fragrant, is Albertine. Possibly the best-loved climbing rose is still Gloire de Dijon, raised in 1853; its creamy-apricot tea-scented blooms are among the first roses to open and among the last to surrender to winter.

A garden—and it can be quite a tiny garden—where old plants

are treasured is a delightful place, green and peaceful, full of soft colours and sweet scents: a garden where you can relax. It is so much more restful than one which is 'a blaze of colour'. Even more, it is a garden where you can work happily and get to know and love the plants and understand their ways: a place where there is always something to do and enjoy.

LOCAL FLOWER NAMES   Jennifer True

Lilacs and laburnums are called Prince's Feathers and Golden Chain in the West. The old man who does odd jobs calls American currant bush Currantariby, wallflowers Bloody Warriors and antirrhinums Snappyjacks. To children the wild daffodil is Lent Lily, the greater stitchwort, Ladies' Wathes and the pink campion and blue vetch, Raggetty Jack and Hen-and-chickens. Bluebells are Cuckoos, bryony and nightshade Pixy Leaves. Creeping toadflax is Pedlars' Baskets, while Drunkards is the name given to the marsh marigold. The big purply cranesbill is called in many districts in North Devon Jacky Jesus. The young red-brown leaves of the oak are known as Chick-chack. The little burrs that cling to one's garments as one walks through rough grass have the name of Clitchy Buttons, the outer coats of the Spanish chestnut are Fuzzy Bears. Daffodils in one parish in North Devon are called Gregories. St Gregory's Day falls during the time they are in flower.

WILD FLOWERS FOR THE GARDEN?
David McClintock

When may we with a clear conscience bring wild flowers into our gardens? There are people who dig them up without a thought, and others who would allow none to be taken. Which is right? How, except by digging, can we try out the enticing suggestions, accompanied by frequent and emphatic counsel of restraint, in W. E. Th. Ingwersen's book, *Wild Flowers in the Gardens*? No fewer than fifteen of the British wild flowers described in

Bentham and Hooker alone are now extinct, and perhaps also summer lady's tresses. (Has any reader of *The Countryman* seen this orchid in Britain during recent years?) So vigilance is essential to prevent further losses. Co-operation has to be sought—and is usually gladly given—from owners on whose land threatened rarities grow. The only remaining locality in Britain for the monkey orchid was recently ploughed by an unwitting farmer; but he was visited before the destruction was complete. The spread of towns cannot, of course, be resisted on this score, but when building is certain the doomed plant may be taken elsewhere: I once attempted this with a rare umbellifer, *Falcaria vulgaris*, at Hayes in Kent. But it is not only the actual smothering of plants by houses that is fatal; the spread of towns threatens the surrounding countryside. A. W. Boyd has recently told how primroses have disappeared from around Northwich, where they have all been dug up, and they are vanishing near London. Drainage and its converse, the making of reservoirs, also endanger wild flowers. Just before the raising of the level of Loch Tummel inundated the only British station for the rare bog-rush *Schoenus ferrugineus*, clumps of it were moved to similar sites near by; a friend and I took some to Loch Rannoch. Animals may trample or eat plants out of existence: the only spot in the British Isles where the snake-tongue crowfoot still grows was bought by the Society for the Promotion of Nature Reserves to save the plant from cows. The making or widening of roads and spraying of verges must be carefully watched. But many see as the worst potential threat to our wild flowers the people who pick or dig them up.

What then should we do if we see a rare wild flower or a fine variety of a common one which we should like to grow ourselves? The best course is usually to get it from a nurseryman. I once listed nearly five hundred British wild flowers in trade catalogues. All were not the typical native forms; some were improved forms more suitable for the garden. But we do not all carry our single-mindedness or patriotism so far that we insist, for example, on the British form of *Linnaea borealis* in preference to the larger and finer (not always the same thing) North American one. Nevertheless it is remarkable how many truly British plants can be so acquired, with the assurance that they will have good roots and a proper chance of survival.

If we cannot buy plants, we may be able to collect or buy seed. Only a small proportion of the seed of a wild plant survives naturally, and there is little risk of our taking it all. What we do collect is likely to produce a positive increase of the species. Furthermore, plants raised from seed are constitutionally more robust than old rooted plants or cuttings. Several nurserymen here and abroad offer seeds of a rich variety of British species. The Royal Horticultural Society distributes seeds free annually to its Fellows, and gardening friends are often useful suppliers.

Another source of supply is cuttings, taken in moderation. These call for skill, but it is the best way to perpetuate choice strains of established plants, particularly shrubs. If they were left alone, their better colour or markings or shape would usually be lost, for natural crossing tends to breed out any such eccentricity by making it improbable that the offspring would repeat the distinction of the maternal parent.

Lastly—absolutely lastly, and not to be undertaken lightly or wantonly—there is digging. Before you dig, always let your conscience be your guide, as well as common sense and knowledge of what is likely to survive and what is too scarce or tricky to attempt. The plant may be rarer than we realise. So often the one we covet is attractive largely because it is in its prime or at its greatest development with an extensive root system. Efforts to move it must at least maul and hamper it, even if it does not have to travel far or need any symbiotic mycorrhiza to its roots. It is rarely advisable to attempt to move a plant when it is in flower. When it is permissible to dig take the youngest plants—best of all, the seedlings, which are not only easier to move and more likely to survive the operation, but in nature stand a greater risk of accidental destruction before they reach maturity.

It is, however, usually best not to dig. Even if you are not embarrassingly caught, your handiwork will leave—to put it mildly —a bad taste. I still remember seeing the holes on Minchinhampton golf course where pasque-flowers had been; and one summer I did not like the look of a trowel left near orchids on the South

Downs. It must be at least partly selfish to take a wild plant for one's own pleasure, let alone for financial profit; and the more frequented the area, the more is digging to be avoided. But where the plant is abundant and blossoms unseen, it surely may be not only permissible, but possibly desirable, to gather it for wider enjoyment. I can instance a remarkable harlequin variety of bell heather, with a broad white stripe horizontally across the centre of each corolla, which I found on the wild southern approaches to Ben Vrackie. This I sent to a famous nursery for propagation, but sadly even they failed to keep it. I regret the failure, but not the attempt.

In my own county of Kent, and I believe in most, if not all, other counties, there are Wild Plant Protection Orders, buttressing the Malicious Damage Act, 1861; both forbid the uprooting of plants. So, if ever you are tempted to dig, remember that you may also fall foul of the law.

UMBELLIFERAE

'*They're a dull lot.*'—Robert Gathorne Hardy
Not to me! When the incoming waves
Of late spring break on the shores,
And I drive my Israelitish chariot
Between high banks of umbelliferae,
It is as if a hand divided the sea.

No botanist, I shall never discover
Which is which of parsley, parsnips,
Chervils, fennels. It was sanicle
I knew and named, finding it first,
Delicate, by the Birks of Aberfeldy.

Let ragwort rage in the waste places,
And the rose-bay willow herb flaunt
Itself along hillsides, and knapweed
Rear its purple head—I am ravished
By suspended waves of umbelliferae,

57

As Socrates might have been, seeing
Hemlock flowing on the Acropolis,
Where he walked, corrupting the youth
Of Athens with questions that smote
The way to a promised Land of Truth.

F. Pratt Green

PINCH AND SMELL   Evelyn Woodforde

A great many plants are what Bacon called fast of their scent, and
of these lemon-verbena is quite my favourite. Since it was first
brought to Britain in 1784, numberless small girls must have been
told to 'pinch and smell, dear', and not one of them can have forgotten the first sudden impact of astringent sweetness.

In Chile, lemon-verbena forms a tree 20ft high; here it is supposed to be unreliable except in the extreme south and south-west.
But plants, like humans, can withstand surprising hardship if they
are happy. A warm, dry soil and a sheltered south wall are what this
verbena likes. It is a nuisance, of course, to remove the two top
spits and mix them with leaf-mould, turfy loam and sand, and then
to fork rough humus into the bottom (third) spit; but if one is to be
rewarded by something desirable, lasting and untroublesome it is
worth while.

Our two plants in Sussex have survived the piercing winters
without special protection for twenty years. One beside the sitting-
room window is clutched in fond embrace by the larger Maiden's
Blush rose. A summer came when it towered luxuriantly above my
head and the apple-green shoots were elegantly tipped with silver-
white flowers. Alas, the following winter outrageous frosts cut back
the main stem, and since then it has never been more than a modest
bush. Litter on the ground and sacking suspended from the wall
above would have been simple and sensible precautions in such
weather. The other verbena, in an unglamorous position by the
clothes-line, has never done so well.

Still, nothing is quite like lemon-verbena: a cool, composed plant, and the very thing to abate the heat of a burning summer's day, as that ingenious gardener, Sir George Sitwell, must have known when he ordained urns of it in his Italian garden at Castello di Montegufoni. The mature leaves, quickly dried over an electric radiator, make a most valuable ingredient for my slapdash pot-pourri brew. In death, curiously enough, they give up their noble essence without so much as a single tweak.

FILLING JUNE GAPS   Rosemary Verey

Bedding-out is an ugly word nowadays, so our wallflowers, tulips, forget-me-nots and polyanthus have to be incorporated into the borders among shrubs and herbaceous plants. Spring would be dull without their colour and delicious scents, but by June their spaces need refilling. This gives an opportunity to introduce a few unusual plants with attractive foliage, particularly if you have a greenhouse or frost-proof shed to winter them. Bold striking leaves can do as much for a border as the usual summer space-fillers like petunias and antirrhinums. For ideas we can turn fruitfully to the writings of that great gardener William Robinson. In 1867, as a young man, he went to Paris as representative of the nursery-garden firm of Veitch and as gardening correspondent for *The Times*. The title of his first book was *Gleanings from French Gardens*. It was the beginning of his lifelong attack on Victorian carpet bedding which eventually had such an overwhelming influence on English style. Inevitably many of his suggestions conjure up the thought of a bowler-hatted head gardener issuing orders to his underlings; but if you reduce his ideas to present-day standards and your own pair of hands, some original suggestions emerge.

He recommended the castor oil plant, *Ricinus*, for a tall bold effect. Most seedsmen sell seeds of this, and one packet will produce a dozen or more plants. Treated as half-hardy annuals and put out in early June, they will grow to 6ft. The handsome palmate leaves are a foot across and vary in colour from dark green to bronze-red. They have stout stems and, in a sheltered position, need no staking. We have grown them for several years, and I am always surprised and delighted with the amount of growth they make. A good foil for their large shiny leaves is *Melianthus major*, an aristocrat with exciting foliage. The glaucous sea-green leaves, with sharply toothed edges, are attractive in every stage of their development, especially as they unfurl, like expanding paper decorations. Their texture invariably lures people to touch them, which is unfortunate, as they have a curious pungent and not altogether pleasant scent. The remedy is to plant a lemon-scented verbena close by. I bought one melianthus plant three years ago and,

Melianthus major

as it was labelled 'half-hardy', dug it up and divided it in the autumn, keeping it in a frost-free greenhouse; and by spring the strong roots had thrown up several new shoots. Now we have a good supply of them, so one plant only goes inside and the others are left out with light protection for the roots.

If you enjoy taking cuttings, the half-hardy variegated abutilon is rewarding. Its leaves are generously marked with yellow, and a small group will lighten a patch between dark-leafed shrubs; it carries a series of attractive orange lantern-shaped flowers throughout the summer. I take cuttings from the side shoots in the autumn, and winter them in the greenhouse. They are ready for potting after a few weeks, and by June have become good sturdy plants up to 18in high, probably already flowering. Once in the border they grow fast, and by autumn will be 4–5ft tall with a yard spread.

All house plants grow out of doors in their natural state, and most welcome a few summer months in the garden. The leaves of the rubber plant, *Ficus elastica*, look twice as handsome outside as they do collecting dust indoors and will, to quote Robinson, 'not only exist in the open air in summer in good health, but make a good growth under the influence of our weak northern sun'. The exotic flowers of the ginger plant, *Hedychium gardnerianum*, have an overbearing scent in the house but, when it is stood outside or sunk in the border in its pot at a strategic distance from where you sit, the smell is marvellous.

Echevarias, too, summer well outside, and the best for a low effect is the compact *E glauca metallica*. The attractive grey-green fleshy leaves are densely clustered in symmetrical rosettes. One

Echevaria glauca metallica

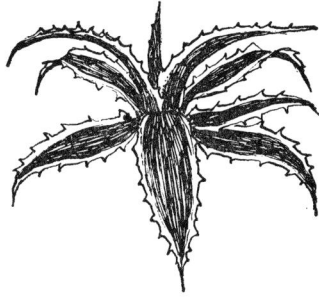

Agave

plant we were given two summers ago was put out in a stone trough where it grew visibly, until by autumn it was 9in across and had formed several new rosettes close to the short main stem. These were pulled off and potted, had soon made roots and were then wintered in a frame. Last summer we put them out in a group on a sunny corner between rock roses where they looked very decorative. They will stand a mild frost, so there is no need to bring them in too early. To my mind they are no more trouble than growing a box of half-hardy plants.

The possibilities are manifold and depend on what you may have in the greenhouse or the increasingly popular gardenroom. Philo-dendrons, fatsias and the green and yellow spider plants all thrive outside in summer. Once you have developed an eye for using interesting foliage, you will find yourself acquiring aloes and agaves, and growing jacaranda and aralia from seed.

A GARDEN OF FRAGRANCE   Roy Genders

At the end of my garden, divided from the usual lawns, rose beds and herbaceous borders by a 6ft wall and a row of silver birches, is an almost square piece of ground about 50ft long. For several years I left it as I found it, overgrown with nettles and couch. Then it came to me one summer evening when the smell of wild honeysuckle filled the air: why not make of this waste plot a garden of fragrance? Through the autumn and winter, while the work of clearing it went on, I made copious notes, so that I had a scheme well in mind before I ordered the plants.

There would be two borders, one herbaceous and the other a shrubbery backed by trees, with a bed of herbs connecting the two at the lower end. A raised bed of Ena Harkness roses would form the centre-piece, set in a lawn surrounded by crazy paving. The plants would have to be perennial, needing as little labour as possible. The garden being small, I would avoid any with a tendency to rampant growth; and as the site was exposed I would have to reject all things tender: several of the highly perfumed magnolias, for example, and those viburnums which are not truly hardy.

For a winter-flowering shrub my first choice was *Viburnum fragrans*, which grows about 6ft high, needs little pruning and carries from November to February white tubular blooms sweetly scented. It would be followed by the little-known *Viburnum carlesii* from Korea. This seldom grows taller than 4ft and is not too happy in soil with lime; nor does it like cold winds. But in the shelter of a hurdle, fence or hedge it bears in early spring a profusion of flowers with carnation scent, especially noticeable after a shower of rain. In late autumn its foliage turns a brilliant scarlet. It is therefore well worth a trial, even though it may not succeed. Another lovely shrub is the evergreen Japanese viburnum, *V henryi*, whose lemon-scented flowers in midsummer are followed by bright red berries.

For winter fragrance I chose also witch-hazel, of which there are several charming species. Possibly the most valuable is *Hammamelis virginiana*, which grows to a height of 10–12ft, producing its pale yellow sweetly scented flowers in October and November, when there is little perfume in the garden. Most of us know the species *mollis*, but *vernalis* is more graceful in habit and its foliage turns an attractive bright yellow in autumn. Small crimson flowers tinged with yellow appear from Christmas until March and carry a powerful perfume, especially enjoyable if a sprig is taken indoors.

Early spring fragrance was to be provided by daphnes. We all know the richly coloured *D mezereum*, though we may despair of its ever reaching a worthwhile size. It was suggested to me that I should plant instead the variety Somerset, in all soils a stronger grower, which bears clusters of bright rosy-pink flowers in May. Its perfume is even stronger than that of *mezereum*.

A little-known but extremely hardy plant that deserves wider recognition is the evergreen *Osmarea burkwoodii*: its box-like foliage is crowded with fragrant white blooms during May, a sparse month in the garden. It does well in any soil and is particularly suitable for a small hedge. In a lime-free soil a most handsome shrub, excellent in a shady corner, is *Pieris forrestii*, which is not only evergreen, with blossom of delicious fragrance, but has the distinction of vivid crimson leaves in summer.

For summer fragrance I decided to include mock orange, *Philadelphus*. Several varieties possess an unpleasantly powerful scent, but the rich Jersey-cream coloured flowers of *P coronarius* have a delicate orange perfume. Belle Etoile produces, on long arching sprays rather like those of a buddleia, white, flushed purple blooms with a fragrance resembling a pineapple's. I would also plant buddleias for their perfume and graceful habit, as abundantly as space permitted.

The lilac hybrids need almost no attention after planting; more lilacs are spoilt by overpruning than any other shrub. They like a soil richer in humus than most and should be left to grow as they will, with ample room for development. As space was limited, I chose five of different colours. First came the new variety Primrose, which bears a profusion of rich yellow blooms that seem to carry a true primrose fragrance; but it has made little progress as yet and may be too slow-growing.

An old favourite, Charles Joly, with long fully double spikes, is still the best of the rich purples, and the strongly perfumed Madame Lemoine the best of the double whites. I also included the double silver-pink Lucie Baltet, the first lilac to flower, and the new pale blue Clarke's Giant, which has the largest flower spikes of any lilac. This completed the shrubbery, lavenders being reserved for the herbaceous border, but to cover a stone arch I planted a winter-sweet, *Chimonanthus fragrans*, to flower from Christmas to March. This may be grown as a small shrub, though it makes quicker growth on a sheltering wall.

As edging for the shrubbery I chose catmint and for the herbaceous border old-fashioned pinks. Both are best planted in early April when they will begin to grow away at once, making large bushy plants by the end of summer. One of the loveliest and most fragrant of the old pinks is Glory of Lyonaise, whose double shell-pink blooms have attractive deep cream centres. Jane Austen is a single of rich mulberry colour, fringed white. The old Victorian may be likened to a cabbage rose, for it bears a huge cabbage-like white bloom, heavily laced jet black, with tremendous perfume. For contrast the glowing double Red Emperor, maroon with crimson eye, is a beauty.

I made lilies the basis of the herbaceous border, planting them in clusters of three with the taller varieties at the back. In April, when I had worked plenty of leaf-mould into the deeply dug soil, I planted the bulbs 8in apart and 6in deep on sand, filling in with peat. I bought only varieties noted for hardiness, easy-doers and quite inexpensive. Toward the back of the border I planted *Lilium regale* and its pure white counterpart; Maxwill for its brilliant orange flowers in late July; the Californian lily, *L pardalinum giganteum*, with its blooms of vivid scarlet and purple markings at the centre; and *L henryi* for August flowering. Several are only slightly fragrant, but all are superb border plants. In front are *L cernuum*, noted for its dainty lilac-pink blooms; two varieties of *L pumilum*, the scarlet one known to our gardens about a hundred years ago and Golden Gleam; and as a contrast *L speciosum album*, a particular favourite of mine with flowers of purest white, striped green, and attractive chocolate-coloured anthers. Lilies bloom year after year, the only attention required being some staking in early summer and a peat mulch after flowering in autumn.

Lavenders were planted in the border during March, the best time for moving them in an exposed garden. I managed to find a dozen, ranging from the dwarf blue, pink and mauve Hidcote varieties, which take a long time to reach a height of 1ft, to the tall Grappenhall, ideal for a hedge and worth growing for its blooms; it is the darkest of all lavenders. Useful as a contrast and almost as vigorous is the pure white variety, *alba*.

One of the most pleasantly perfumed of all plants is the Chilean *Verbena corymbosa*, which seems quite hardy in Britain if a few fronds of bracken are placed over the roots during severe weather. These spread with great freedom and it quickly forms a large bushy plant which is covered in late summer with a mass of flowers carrying the true verbena scent. Bergamots, too, are deliciously aromatic and require just an ordinary soil and no staking. The clear rose Croftway Pink and the dark crimson Mahogany, keep excellent company with the more common but equally lovely Cambridge Scarlet. I planted with them in groups the violet-blue garden sage, *Salvia nemorosa*. A rare plant, easily grown, is *Delphinium brunonianum*, a native of the Himalayas. It produces on 2ft stems flowers of palest sky-blue, and its strangely hairy foliage has a rich musk aroma that is especially pronounced after a July shower. With it I have planted the sweetly perfumed peony, Duchesse de Nemours, its large double creamy-white flowers being, in midsummer, as lovely as their perfume. About the border are masses of *Iris reticulata*, which produces scented violet-and-orange flowers in late winter.

The small herb garden was included because of its value in the kitchen, as well as its fragrance outdoors and in. Rosemary and hyssop; sage and lemon thyme; the camphor plant and eau-de-Cologne mint, with chamomile in the gaps between the crazy paving, for the more it is trodden, the more it exhales its fragrance. A herb garden is a story to itself, but try drying the leaves of eau-de-Cologne mint with those of rosemary or white bergamot and hanging them in a small muslin bag in the bedroom. They will fill it with the most delightful fragrance for many weeks.

UPLAND GARDEN   Margaret Mitchell

It was the snowdrops that brought us here. Thousands of them on the braeside sloping down to the burn reminded us of our first home in the Lakes. We could not resist them. So here we are in our upland garden, battling with a climate which is frustrating to any keen gardener. The cottage lies 900ft up on a bare ridge on the

The cottage high up on the Peebleshire Border

Peebleshire border, and the garden had long been neglected. We started off enthusiastically, clearing many yards of stubborn snowberry and dealing with rank upon rank of nettles that stood breast-high and completely cut us off from the eastern end of the garden. After these our worst enemies were couch grass, bishopweed and buttercup. When we took down a hedge of blackcurrant and raspberry close to the house, we discovered a rustic flight of stone steps and a lovely old stone wall, which was sprouting yet more enemies. But at long last the garden was cleared.

The first shock came when we went to order flowering shrubs.

66

The nurseryman looked at us sadly and said, 'You can't grow any-thing up at Ridgehill'. In the end he invited us to give him a list of our preferences, and undertook to select those trees and shrubs most likely to do well at our impossible altitude. But we had had enough; we placed orders with our favourite nurserymen, two in the 'deep south' and two in the 'frozen north'. We cannot say that the plants from the south do any worse than those from our northern suppliers, in spite of the advice, often given, to buy always from firms farther north than your own garden.

In four years ours has at last been established: paths laid, grass sown, shrubs planted and a small rock garden begun. The vege-table plot is perhaps the easiest part. The soil, untilled for many years, grows good potatoes, peas, beans and the usual roots, also summer brassicas. But it is not worth our while to attempt winter-standing crops such as sprouts, spring cabbage and perpetual spinach, because of frost and bitter east winds in spring, which do more damage than all the winter cold.

The primula family does well, and violas come up undismayed year after year. Early summer is no problem with easy plants: campanula, lupin, oriental poppy, columbine, Jacob's ladder, dame's violet, to mention but a few. Full summer is more difficult, as carnations and chrysanthemums just will not bloom in time. Pinks have to be lifted and over-wintered in a frame. There is not sun enough for successful annuals. Dahlias flourish until the first frost; but every month may have its share. We used to say that July was a summer month; but even it has sometimes let us down, and by mid-August we must expect sharp nights.

The worst casualties of the long winter and bitter winds and frosts of early spring are the roses. As they are our favourite flowers, they were the first plants we bought, cheerfully ordering all those varieties which had blossomed so abundantly for us in Edinburgh. Planted in April, they did wonderfully well the first summer, and we laughed at the nurseryman's gloomy forecast. But we have learnt that it is never wise to discount local knowledge, for the first winter's severity cut our roses to ground level; and that is their fate every year. We have tried all the methods we can devise to shelter them: earth mounded round the stems, a deep litter of bracken and, one winter in despair, a shelter of strong hessian. Can anyone advise us how to grow roses at 900ft?

The shrub roses do better than HT's and floribundas, but even they cannot give of their best. Hardiest seem to be the rugosas such as Conrad Meyer and Roseraie de l'Hay, and the Scots briar, *R spinosissima* hybrids, including Harrisonii and Stanwell's Perpetual. Even the ramblers, always considered to be fully hardy, suffer from winter's freezing touch. Our larch poles and ropes seem unlikely to have to support a weight of foliage and blossom. One ray of sunshine however: no hardship can suppress the fine old *R alba semiplena*, the Jacobite rose. So we struggle on, each year trying a few more varieties, hoping to discover those that will face up to arctic conditions. And when the hedges of beech and myrobolan have grown thick enough to sift the wind, to take the first edge from its scorching passage, who knows?

Is the game worth the candle? Yes, we think so. It is a constant challenge, and hope springs eternal. Meanwhile we have taken the advice Sir Walter Scott's Laird of Dumbiedikes gave to his son: 'When ye hae naething else to do, ye may be ay sticking in a tree: it will be growing when ye're sleeping.' We are always sticking in trees, and in our damp and somewhat sunless climate they grow with abandon. Birch, beech, larch and poplar are better bets than roses and the more fastidious flowering trees and shrubs. As compensation for the absence of blossom and of hot summer days when you must sit in the shade we have the clear invigorating upland air, the wild call of curlew on the pasture, and the bonny hills encircling our little garden.

GLADIOLI FROM SEED   W. Ewart Bull

In our garden in a valley of the Low Peak district one of our happiest ventures has been the growing of gladioli from seed gathered from selected flower-spikes in our own borders. The complete process takes four years, so patience is needed; but the method is quite simple and the probability of success high. I am not referring to controlled hybridisation and the raising of new named varieties, which are tasks for the professional, but to the growing of corms from naturally fertilised and ripened seed.

The parent stock was of sound quality: we made sure that bees had something good to work on before we left them to cross-pollinate in their own way. It is not every season that seed ripens well in our hill district, but we were able to gather the pods in October, dry them off thoroughly and rub out the round seed. This we sowed in the early spring in boxes with a covering of loam. The greenhouse was slightly warmed, and the grass-like seedlings appeared after two or three weeks, the percentage of germination being high. As the leaves gained strength, the tiny corms began to swell and we put the boxes in a sunny position in the open when the danger of frost had passed, though a touch of frost will do no harm. Through the summer we kept the boxes watered. In a very hot spell they should be shaded; otherwise they may dry out, when the corms will stop growing and ripen prematurely. Ours went on growing until the early autumn, and we then left them to dry off before shaking the soil from their roots and storing them for the winter.

The second spring we planted the corms in inch-deep drills in rich, well-cultivated ground where they would have full sun. A lively vigour was quickly noticeable in the leaves and there were several flower shoots, which we cut off. Any seedling that showed signs of yellowing during growth was destroyed. When we lifted the corms that autumn they were half-grown, and again we stored them in the dry. The third year we set them out in drills 2in deep and allowed the flower shoots to remain. Some delightful colours and delicate shades were revealed, but of greater interest to us was the strength of the plants compared with others in the garden.

Most produced not only flowers but large corms for planting the fourth year—this time in the best borders, where they made a glorious display in a dry summer with shoots up to 6ft high. They also grew massive corms rich in colour and texture. I commend the venture to other countrymen who seek not the florist's perfection but the gardener's delight.

LINES FOR A COUNTRY GARDEN

The quality of light within this garden,
As from a concentration here, has grown
So rich, it is as if the air has taken
Gold from the sun or silver from the moon
And holds them finely particled in one
Suspended pouring that is never done.

So in the sunlight now this cherry-bark
Glows like old leather, and warmth equally
Lies hidden in the wallflower's velvet dark
Or blazes from the lilac's lazuli;
Even the rust upon this wrought-iron seat
Is turned to burnish by the golden heat.

And surely this shall last when they are gone
Who kept this garden. If love can endure
Shall it not do so here, something work on,
Making its own memorial of air?
Something that says: This is a place to bless,
Though all the world return to wilderness.

D. J. Sutton

A GARDEN POND IN THE MAKING

A. D. Imms, DSC FRS

It was in 1933 that we decided a pond would add to the amenities of our Cambridgeshire garden. During the winter the gardener was given a sketch similar to that shown and was deputed to make the necessary excavation, after the area had been marked out with sticks and string on a small, unwanted piece of lawn. The walls were to be vertical to a depth of six inches, and then to slope inwards slightly. This slope was a provision against the pressure of ice cracking the walls of the pond, for ice would tend to slide upwards a little as it formed. During twelve East Anglian winters, several of which were

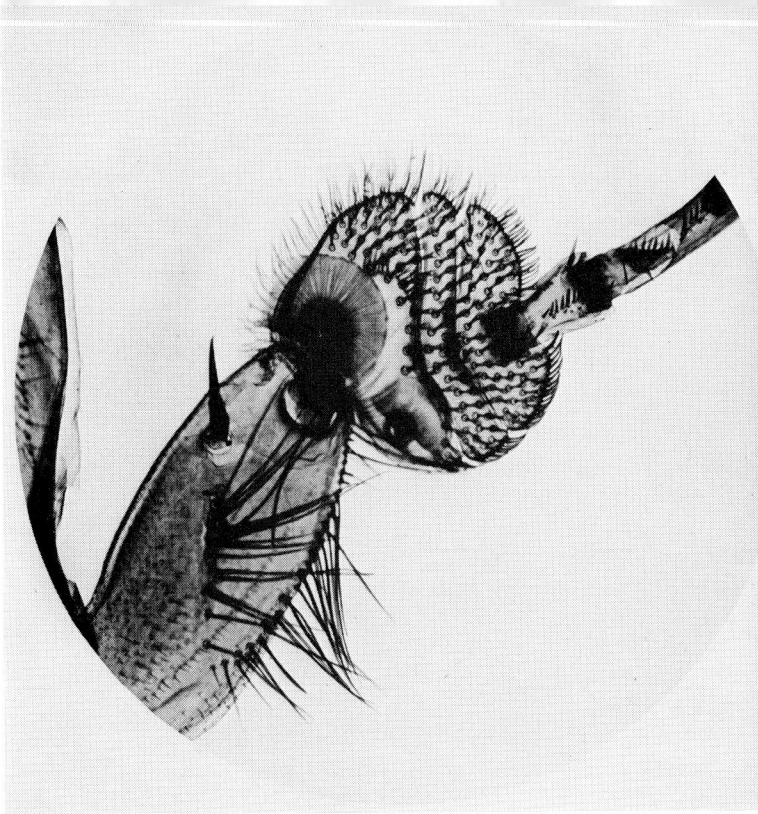

Page 72 (left) Banana squash from California; *(below)* Popular American Hubbard Squash with its dark green, warty skin

severe to an unusual degree, no cracks appeared. The depth of the excavation varied from two to three and a half feet, as shown in the sketch. A small jobbing builder concreted the floor and walls. The concrete was four inches thick, and the walls were reinforced with pieces of old iron-wire netting and iron rods; an old bedstead was embedded in the floor.

One problem was to prevent the alkali in the cement dissolving in the water, to the detriment of the life of the pond. This was done by coating the whole inside surface with a proprietary waterproofing substance. When the pond had been filled for a week, a kindly friend, a research chemist by profession, analysed a sample of the water and pronounced it no different, in its chemical composition, from the local supply.

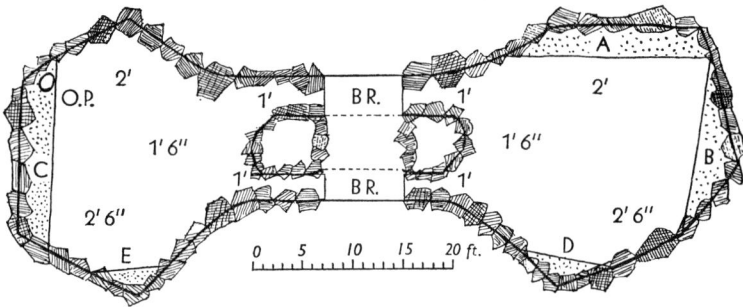

Garden pond in the making

Once the requisite balance of animal and plant life had been established, the pond would become stabilised, as it were, and would never be interfered with, so that no provision was made for emptying. The overflow is an iron pipe (OP) rising one inch above the usual level of the water when the pond is full.

There are five pockets for soil in different parts of the pond. Pockets A and B have the soil level with the surface of the water when the pond is full. The soil in pocket C is two inches below the water level, that in D nine inches, and that in E fifteen inches below. In the confining walls of the first three pockets, six half-inch glass tubes were inserted in the cement during construction to allow free entry of the water into the soil. The bottom of the pond was covered with a four-inch layer of fine loam, with two inches of gravel over it to prevent fish from nosing into the soil and thereby making the water turbid. The 'island' in the middle of the pond is connected with the 'mainland' by two bridges (BR) made of single slabs of stone. Pieces of limestone and sandstone rock are set irregularly into the top of the concrete all around the pond, some rocks projecting over the water more than others. In this way the hard artificial lines of the concrete walls are concealed. In the pockets of soil flanking the rocks, we planted aubrietias of different kinds, sedums, arabis, arenaria and other plants which draped the rocks and hung over the edge down to the surface of the water.

The next step was to stock the pond with water-plants and to ensure that these were properly established before any fish were introduced. Of first importance are submerged oxygenating plants that serve to keep the water well aerated for fish and other animals. The giant anacharis, *Elodea crispa* was given first place for this purpose, since it grows rapidly and is evergreen. A stone was tied at the cut end of a small bunch of stems, so that the whole sank to the bottom and rooting soon took place. Other oxygenating plants established were water milfoil, hornwort and water starwort. Filamentous algae, or so-called 'blanket-weed', proved troublesome towards midsummer, when it choked up much of the pond and restricted the movements of the fish. The dragging along the water-surface of a small cotton bag, containing about half a pound of copper sulphate, was a successful remedy, but it had to be repeated several times in a season. Later, strands of stout copper wire were stretched across the pond at several points and at different depths below the surface. Apparently the small amount of copper continuously dissolved in the water was sufficient to check any subsequent algal growth.

The blooms of the double marsh marigold, in pocket A, were a most attractive sight in spring. In front of them, and dipping into the water, was a rampant growth of *Mimulus variegata*. Cotton grass, *Eriophorum angustifolium*, flourished in pocket B; also flowering rush, which ultimately died out, and the lovely blue water iris, *I laevigata*. In pocket C there was a vigorous growth of bog-bean and water forget-me-not; and water hawthorn, *Aponogeton distachyum*, sent up its large racemes of white blossoms, with their coal-black anthers, above the water in pocket D, usually twice a year. In pocket E grew a large plant of the golden club, *Orontium aquaticum*, in company with the double Japanese arrowhead. In the middle of each main division of the pond a small water-lily was submerged, with its roots in a basket. The two kinds chosen were the white sweet-scented *Nymphaea odorata minor* and the rosy-purple-flowered *N purpurata*.

Most of the plants flourished exceedingly in their surroundings, and many had to be severely restricted. About a wheelbarrow-load of giant anacharis was removed every year to keep it within bounds. The golden club had literally to be torn up as it tended to choke the Japanese arrowhead towards the end of each summer. Many leaves were removed from the water-lilies to allow light and air to penetrate the water. Also, it was found that if they were allowed to produce too much leaf the blossoms were relatively few. When checked in this way the white-flowered lilies often produced more than fifty blossoms in a season. For some unexplained reason, water violet never flourished, although it grew normally in the fenland dikes.

No attempt was made to keep to the rule of one inch of fish per gallon of water. Instead, in several thousand gallons, a start was made with six golden rudd, nine golden orfe (five inches long) and six small goldfish. Afterwards a few native carp and tench were added, to help to keep the water as fresh as possible, as they function largely as bottom scavengers. Six thunder fish were also added for the same purpose. These curious loaches are eel-like in form and have the habit of rushing to the surface, taking in a gulp of air, and disappearing again during thundery weather. Of the six kinds of fish the golden orfe is by far the most attractive. Almost peach-coloured, it swims actively close to the surface and, where there are several, they keep together in shoals. They rise freely to take insects, often leaping out of the water. At night we used to hear them fall back again with a resounding plop. The goldfish are more sluggish. They display themselves less, and are in general less attractive creatures. The thunder fish were hardly ever seen, and after growing to nearly two feet in length—judging from a dead specimen fished up along with weed—they seem to have died out. Goldfish, golden rudd and golden orfe all bred freely. The parents, in most cases, seem to relish feeding off their young, of which only a few survive each year.

Of invertebrate animals, about a hundred water-snails, *Planorbis* and *Limnaea*, were introduced. They were fed upon by the larger fishes and did not seem to increase in numbers. The brown fresh water hydra was very abundant some years on the undersides of water-lily leaves, especially when the leaves were attacked by larvae of a chironomid midge. The hydras fed eagerly upon the very young larvae, so that they became progressively scarcer.

The other insect life of the pond would require a whole article to describe adequately. The commonest insects that established themselves were small may-flies, pond skaters, water-boatmen, dragonfly nymphs, great water-beetles, and their smaller relative, *Acilius sulcatus*. There were many other creatures of more particular interest to the entomologist. Great water-beetles were removed from the pond whenever they were seen, because they are far too prone to prey upon the smaller fish (see picture on page 71). Other predators, of a larger kind, happily did not include cats. A heron paid only a single, hurried visit, and left with a goldfish. A kingfisher, on the other hand, paid several leisurely visits, perching on a particular rock in apparent contemplation of the fish life, although it was never seen to dive into the water.

We enjoyed the pond and its seasonal changes for some twelve years, until we had to leave Cambridgeshire. What has happened to it since it passed out of our keeping, we have not inquired.

VEGETABLES YOU MIGHT GROW   B. G. Furner

My work necessitates the growing of many vegetables which are seldom seen in most kitchen-gardens, and trials in my Kentish garden include varieties from all over the world. Most striking perhaps are the squashes, hanging on vines trained to the garden fence. The largest is the banana squash from California, 24in long.

Other interesting ones, grown for winter storing, are the Hubbard's dark green with warty skin, and the striped Golden Delicious. Smaller, but even more odd, are the bottle-shaped butter-nuts (see pictures on pages 72, 89). Zucchini and Caserta, two Italian summer squashes popular in the United States, produce good crops of succulent marrows on compact bush plants. I reserve at least one for the production of courgettes—those tasty immature marrows which are becoming popular here. Another vegetable which is finding a ready sale during the summer months is the sweet pepper. I raise my plants in the cold greenhouse, setting them out in the cold frame in early June. The earliest or king pepper is ready for picking in late July; and cropping continues until October. Sweet peppers are much hardier than aubergines, which I also grow, and quite as easy to produce as tomatoes.

Thanks to the kindness of British, American and Japanese seedsmen, as well as of the All Union Institute in Leningrad, I grow a varied selection of melons. One of the best for flavour is the rather odd American banana melon. A smaller one, being grown for the first time in many British gardens this summer, is the new Japanese melon Sweetie. I put it on trial in the cold greenhouse last season and was most impressed with the flavour; it reminded me of a honeydew melon. Unless the summer is a really warm one, the production of water-melons is difficult without some form of artificial heat. I have found only one variety which I consider of any use at all in a cold house, and that is Bunyard's F1 Hybrid—a small, really delicious melon from Japan. My cucumbers are also seen more commonly in Japan and China than in Kent. The handsome plants are trained to a 6ft high trellis, and the rich bed is mulched with wheat straw to retain soil moisture. Although the shorter 12in varieties such as Kaga, Kariha and Ochiai Long Day are more prolific, visitors are always drawn to plants of Chinese Long Improved and Suyo, on which hang cucumbers 20in long.

The large juicy tomatoes preferred by the rest of the world are still not popular in Britain. Readers who have enjoyed these slicing tomatoes in Europe or America may like to grow Town Talk, a large-fruited variety which originated in Nepal. Not only do the bright red, evenly shaped fruits weigh up to 12oz each on outdoor plants, but the crop is good and the flavour remarkable. Self-stopping dwarf bush varieties make a useful edging alongside the garden path. The plants require no stakes, but straw should be tucked under the unripe trusses in July. One of the best varieties is Tiny Tim, bred by the University of New Hampshire. The plants are loaded with cherry-size tomatoes in August and September, and I often suggest them for a window-box.

Many readers will have enjoyed Continental yellow-fleshed potatoes on holidays abroad. I grow several varieties and recommend Blue Eigenheimer for chipping and Fir Apple for salads. Sweet potatoes, *Ipomoea batatas*, require artificial heat. I import rooted cuttings from Texas and plant them on ridged beds in cold frames. The plants make a mass of attractive foliage on 3ft vines, and the tubers are lifted in October. No artificial heat is required for peanuts, if the hardy variety Early Spanish is grown. To give them an early start, I sow the nuts in pots in the cold greenhouse in late April and transfer the plants to their growing positions in the cold frame in early June. After flowering, the small yellow blooms drop to leave what our American friends call the 'peg', which grows downwards and enters the soil alongside the plant. The nuts are produced on the peg below soil level, and that is why peanuts are also known as ground-nuts.

While living in Germany I developed a taste for kohlrabi, which is at its best when no larger than a tennis ball. The plants stand up well to drought conditions, and a regular supply is obtained from sowings at intervals from spring to July. Sweet corn is no longer unusual in Britain, but relatively few gardeners grow their own pop-corn. The plants are raised and cultivated in the same way as those of sweet corn; but the cobs are not harvested till late autumn, when the husks have a paper-like texture. Hang the cobs in a warm room for four weeks before popping the hard grains.

I make two sowings of Bavarian radish. The first, in early April, results in a mass of seed-pods for adding to salads in July and August. From the second sowing in July, I lift some fine radishes in the autumn. Equal in flavour to the Bavarian is the Japanese radish All Season, seeds of which are also sown in July. Not only are visitors astonished at seeing the top 6in or 7in of the roots protruding from the soil, but also at the size of the large roots, each weighing about 6lb.

THE ACCOMMODATING ESCALLONIAS Jack Levett

There are few groups of shrubs more thoroughly accommodating than the charming family whose name commemorates the Spanish botanist Escallon. Although some of these lovely plants have gained a reputation for tenderness and have been unjustly neglected as a result, they will flourish even in our bleaker counties, given a little protection under a wall. As seaside shrubs they have a vigour and ebullience matched by few other plants, and the indifference of some species to smog and soot makes them an ideal choice for town gardens. They make excellent hedges, clipped close, and trained on a wall they will often rise to 10ft or more. The whole family ask for little more than regular and systematic pruning, for the whisper that some species and varieties are shy bloomers can usually be traced back to a reluctance to use the knife. Soil is of little importance, and indeed rich soils seem to inhibit these plants and lead to tender growth. In chalky, stony soil they will withstand the hardest winter.

The lovely and exuberant *E macrantha* with its glossy green, aromatic foliage is still, for my money, the most rewarding of the group. If some nurserymen omit it from their lists, because it is less hardy than some other species, it is still worth getting despite any small trouble it may give you. In the west country it makes splendid hedges and responds so amiably to pruning that it can be kept at any height. In colder districts, if the frosted tops are clipped back in spring, it will quickly push up a crop of fresh flowering shoots. It is a generous plant, giving an abundance of rich rose-red panicles from June right through to October. For less adventurous spirits *E ingramii* makes a practically frost-free wind-break. This tall grower has not quite the same summer splendour as the previous shrub, but in all other respects it is very similar. *E philippiana* is not often stocked, for it is the one species of the family which sheds its leaves in winter. Yet, crowned with masses of small white flowers in midsummer, it will enhance the beauty of any shrubbery or border.

Of the varieties, C. F. Ball is a joy to all who grow it; its velvet crimson flowers seem almost fluorescent in the sunshine. It is a compact variety, with the broad foliage of *E macrantha*. Apple Blossom is a more recent introduction with masses of pink-and-white flower clusters and all the old family charm. But of all the beauties of the hybridists I value most the products of the Donard nurseries. One of the first of these to arrive in our garden was Donard Seedling and it is still one of the best. Another, with much larger flowers but still the same fine shade of apple-blossom pink, is Slieve Donard. Probably the richest coloured of the Donards is Brilliance, which bears its bright carmine flowers on typical, arching, graceful stems.

Even in the rock garden the escallonias have a place. For the bolder parts *E montana*, a delightful evergreen shrub, carries masses of bright fuchsia-red blossom with great charm. *E rubra pygmaea* is a real miniature, barely a foot in height—a thick little bush with vivid blood-red flowers. It is exceptionally long-flowering and seldom troubled by frosts. One of the many advantages of the family is this ability of most species to go on giving flowers long after most other plants. They love the sunshine and respond magnificently to it, but they throw no fit if placed in the shade. I have seen them blooming well where other plants simply go spindly.

Propagation presents no problem. All escallonias strike well in cool moist soil, particularly if a little silver sand is added. Late summer is the best time, for then they can be put out in the open and will root quickly. Pruning is best done in April, when the older main flowering branches should be cut back to about half their length. All dead wood should, of course, be removed, and it sometimes helps to cut out an older branch here and there at ground level. This will assist the nicely balanced growth which is one of the escallonia's most attractive features.

ROCKERY FERNS   G.M.B.

The amateur and even the more experienced gardener is rarely successful with ferns without the special quality of sympathetic hands. He is inclined to dump the ferns in any odd corner that needs 'filling up,' and then to cover them with earth like any ordinary plant, with the result that the poor creatures cannot breathe in comfort.

A fern requires very little soil. It should for preference be planted where its roots can be held in place with stones, and be given just enough soil for nourishment. Alternatively, it must be planted with its 'crown' well above the surrounding earth; otherwise rain will soak into the roots without being able to drain off.

Ferns like plenty of shade and moisture; hence they grow almost always on the north side of a wall. The real fern-lover can grow almost every variety of fern in the open air, at any rate in the south of England—even maidenhair and haresfoot, usually relegated to the greenhouse. True, the former will coarsen in the open, but it will spread abundantly once it takes hold, and it is a lovely sight in spring as the tiny red fronds uncurl.

A well-made rockery is an attraction in any garden. It should have a place entirely to itself, well-shaded and if possible with a stream or fountain in its midst. (*Asplenium marinum*—the sea-fern —must have spray to delight its heart.) River sand makes the perfect path for the rockery, but where space has to be considered, a slope, or any odd corner, may be adapted.

The would-be fern-grower may need some specific directions for planting:

Maidenhair. Lay roots on a fine leaf-mouldy and gravelly soil, placing stones for the roots to creep under.

Scale Fern, *Ceterach*; Wall-rue, *Ruta muraria*: Spleenwort, *Trichomanes*. These little ferns must be placed by themselves, otherwise the larger ferns will overgrow them. If possible, make a mound of small stones, first two or three layers of stones, then roots of ferns horizontally, then another layer of stones direct on the roots. If lime rubble is obtainable, always put it on the roots, underneath the stones.

Asplenium adiantum uigrum. Plant as above but not with them and not where they will be overgrown.

Shield-ferns and Hart's-tongues. These can be planted together and are very easy to grow. If hart's-tongue fronds are erect, instead of bending over, the situation is not sufficiently shady and the soil not entirely suitable.

Lady-ferns. To be effective, give up a big place at the foot of the rockery entirely to them.

Male-ferns. Plant promiscuously between shield-ferns, with hart's-tongues interspersed.

If you are lucky enough to have any roots of *Osmunda,* the king of ferns, they should be planted at the base of any rock-work, more or less in a pit, where the ground is always moist. Soil should be peaty, or at any rate have plenty of leaf-mould of considerable depth. Again, if you can get hold of the lovely Ostrich-fern (an Australian importation), with its graceful plumes and handsome centre seed-frond, put it by itself, as it spreads very rapidly. Also, as its fronds are brittle, take care to plant where there is complete shade, and the least possible wind.

Soil: any leaf-mould, with gravel. Take care that the crown is well above the soil level. With care and attention, the ferns will spread rapidly.

SCHEMING GARDENER   Frances Newman

'You should have seen it last week!' Who has not walked round a garden as the owner wistfully describes the colour schemes torn up by wind, rain or scorching sun? To avoid such disappointments, consider the whole plant and, where the flowers are attractive, think of them as an added bonus. The Japanese go so far as to remove flower buds, I am told, to avoid spoiling the look of a plant. I do not suggest such drastic measures, but group plants where their qualities of foliage, colour and general shape will be complemented by their neighbours', and where the effect will last for as long as possible.

If you choose evergreens, so much the better; the scheme will then give pleasure throughout the year. On the grand scale there is always interest and colour in the evergreen trees and shrubs at Westonbirt Arboretum and, though most of us work on a smaller plan, we can still pick up points. At Abbotswood near Stow-on-the-Wold some evergreens are placed purely as a background and foil for more colourful trees. The sycamore *Acer pseudo-platanus brilliantissimum*, with unusual salmon-pink foliage in spring, is planted directly in front of a group of yews with breath-taking effect. This sycamore forms a neat pyramid-shaped head and is slow-growing, so it is suitable for small gardens. Hollies or conifers could be substituted for the yews.

In my own garden I use lavender in quantity and find it has all the qualities I seek: leaves of pleasant colour all the year, a good shape if trimmed regularly, and deliciously scented flowers to attract humble bees. I grow the old variety Hidcote Blue and Twinkle Purple, which is a slightly larger plant. The dwarf

Cotoneaster congesta nana

cotoneaster, *C congesta nana*, which turns a very dark red in winter, silver dianthus and variegated euonymus look well with them at all times. *Euonymus radicans variegata*, content in sun or shade, makes slow-growing ground cover and is best set out in groups of three or more plants; it will also climb if placed against a wall. Most dwarf conifers associate well with lavender. I have *Picea albertiana conica*, which forms a dense bright green cone, and the grey-green *Juniperus sabina hetzii*, which has an attractive way of putting out long fingers of growth.

Silver-leaved plants are popular, but less use is made of the golden-leaved. The dullest corner, planted with golds, will appear to be bathed in perpetual sunshine. In the gold garden at Hidcote your eyes rise from the ground covered in golden creeping Jenny, *Lysimachia nummularia aurea*, to *Alchemilla mollis* with its foamy yellowish-green flowers, then to a shining pillar of light in the

Acaena microphylla

background—golden hop, *Humulus lupulus aureus*, trained round an upright support. As you enter the little garden, enclosed by high hedges of hornbeam, you are almost dazzled by the brilliance of colour and reflected sunlight from what are, in the main, foliage plants.

Ideally all soil should be covered with plant growth; large bare patches of earth are unattractive, unnatural and wasted opportunities to a keen plantsman or woman. This is not to say that an uncontrolled jungle is any better. You should be able to see the groupings and appreciate the textures in a border. To let one member run wild and invade others is undesirable and difficult to deal with in a short space of time.

All the New Zealand burrs have colourful foliage and cover the ground to a delicate inch; but some must be used with caution in small beds as they are invasive. *Acaena buchananii* has delicate silvery-green leaves and can be planted safely almost anywhere. *A microphylla* has a looser habit with brownish-green colouring and tends to be a spreader best seen under trees or in very large borders. *A novae zaelandiae* has small bronze-coloured leaves and red burrs. They can all be useful on awkward banks and under trees and shrubs. In my own garden they grow in stony ground under a robinia tree, and in spring dwarf daffodils poke a way through them into the early sunshine.

MIDSUMMER

Already now young autumn clenches
Small mailed fists among the chestnut branches.
Spring's candles flickered out in the long light
Of May. The soft bright
Leaves have hardened and grown dark.
As yet unseen
The shining brown-eyed urchins lurk
Behind the green,
While in the tree-top sleeps the old
Rake, the November wind,
His withered hand
Itching to spend the yellow gold.

Edith Roseveare

TAIL CORN

West-country gardener, looking at a row of very stunted broad beans which his employer had sown: 'I'm sorry for your bees, sir; they'll get sore knees sucking 'em'.

AUTUMN

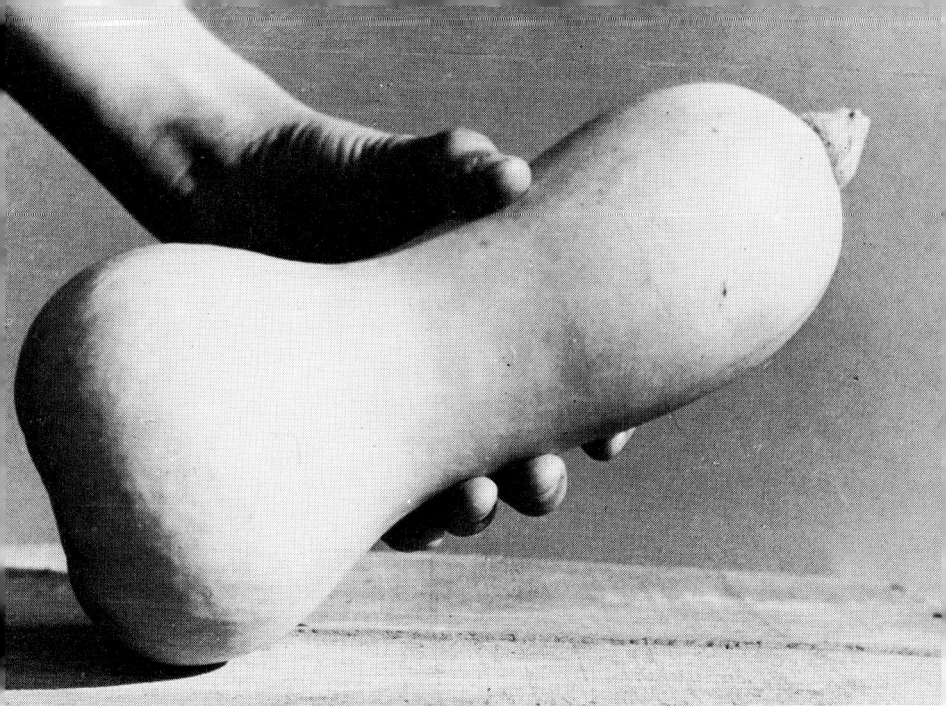

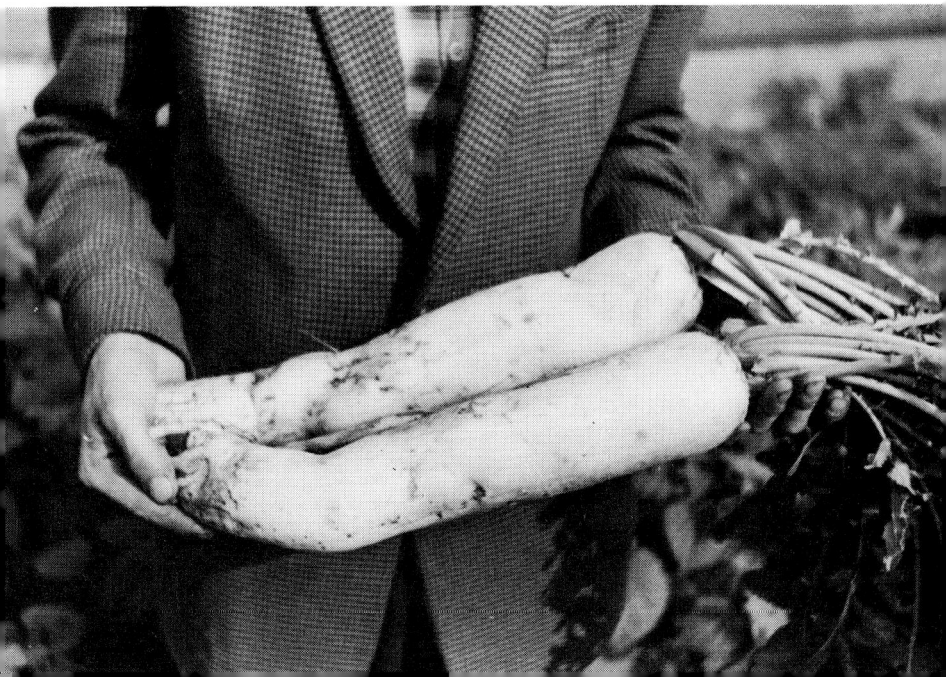

Page 90 (above) Sorbus domestica, from Nash's History of
Worcestershire, 1781; (below) Helleborus corsicus

INDIAN MARIGOLDS

Golden-eyed and burning with the flame
Of many suns, their brittle smell
Pungent and irrepressible:
Emblems of vivid warmth,
Discs of spikiness,
Thick buds pregnant with fires
To burn my plot with splendour.
I love their strength,
The persistence of their growth,
Their splendid pride
And their shining in the night
Like many candles.
I would have a bed so big
That it would dazzle
The bright sun itself.
Such flowers are fit
To crown Arjuna
Or weave a girdle
For the waist of fluting Krishna.

Richard A. Georg

THE PLANT AND THE PLACE   Valerie Finnis

If every garden has its problem corner, there is nearly always the
compensation of a site with something special to offer. As I look
over a wall, or walk round a garden open to the public, I am always
delighted to see a plant that demands attention because it revels in
a site chosen with imagination. In early March I saw a magnificent
shrub of *Viburnum grandiflorum*. It had larger flowers of a deeper
pink and, if anything, more sweetly scented than *V fragrans*. There
it stood, a little apart, covered in bloom and with chionodoxas
beneath. The ground was rising, so I could look up and enjoy the
flowers against a spring sky of palest blue. When I walked round to

the other side, it was almost as impressive with a dark conifer for back cloth. Another exciting sight was a *Daphne cneorum eximia* nearly 5ft across, covered in May with deep pink, sweetly scented blooms—a true 'garland flower'. What a shame it is that so many gardeners are almost frightened of growing daphnes, because they are comparatively easy and tolerate lime. They are perhaps at their best when planted on a low wall. There the drainage is perfect and, when the aubrietia and yellow alyssum are over, the daphne fills the gap before the rockroses and garden pinks come into flower.

On a south-facing wall *Actinidia kolomikta* caught my eye. It had climbed some 20ft and appeared from a distance to be covered with deep pink flowers, though in fact the colour was in the tips of the leaves. This plant, which keeps its colour all through the summer, will grow equally well on a north, east or west wall; but it is in the sun that the leaves turn the richest pink. The scent of honeysuckle on a summer evening is quite heavenly, and it is a great disappointment that one of the best-looking scarlet honeysuckles *Lonicera sempervirens* has no scent at all. I have it growing on a north-east grey stone wall where, for two months this summer, it was weighed down with flowers. A happy solution was to grow the ordinary *Lonicera periclymenum* on the other side of the wall, so that its scent drifts over the top. The number of large-flowered clematis increases each year; but I do not always succeed with them and am more and more attracted to the small-flowered species. Climbing over a little Cotswold garden-shelter, *C orientalis* looked perfectly charming. It is called the orange-peel clematis; its deep yellow flowers with petals resembling thick peel hang nodding from August to October. Once established, it will grow to 10ft or 20ft.

Less happy was a drift of silver birches underplanted with large begonias. How much better it would have been to choose one of the hardy cyclamens! In late summer the delicate flowers of *Cyclamen neapolitanum* would echo the fragility of the trees, and the marbled ivy leaves would provide attractive ground cover from spring to autumn. Plants that flourish under trees are always in demand. Old as it is, Solomon's Seal remains one of the most graceful; I saw it thriving under the dense cover of a large and ancient walnut tree. Also quite happy there was false spikenard, *Smilacina racemosa*, a distinguished plant with creamy-white spikes 3ft long which is at home among hostas and hellebores.

The tiresome small bed near the house, where it may be draughty or shady, defeats many gardeners. Why not try *Helleborus corsicus* there? The large clusters of great apple-green saucer flowers last from December till about the end of May; and splendid great leaves appear to furnish the corner for the rest of the year. The plant seeds itself around and will tolerate almost any soil condition. On the other side of the house, where the tiresome bed is hotter and drier, the rue *Ruta graveolens* Jackman's Blue is invaluable; it looks attractive all the year and is an excellent foil for other plants. So, too, is lady's mantle. The most beautiful downy grey-green fan-shaped leaves and 18in sprays of tiny pale green flowers look good in any tiresome corner or as an edging. Charming in a vase with flowers of all colours, it also dries well for winter decoration.

In April there was a sad gap in many rock gardens, when the early saxifrages and species bulbs were over and the main splash of colour was still to come. In one, hardy European primulas just filled the interval. The bed, made from old mortar rubble and soil, was angled to the north, and between carefully placed rocks the primulas were revelling in their cool root position; the flowers like to be in the sun. *Primula marginata*—imagine a dwarf auricula—has attractively scalloped leaves and mauve flowers; *P m* Linda Pope has much the same colouring but a slightly larger flower; in yellow there is the small hybrid Blairside Yellow, and *P pubescens* Christine is a good cherry-red. I once heard these plants described as having great style, and they certainly look good all the year round. *Potentilla fruticosa arbuscula* will fill almost any flowering gap with large yellow flowers, 2in across, which are a cheerful sight from May to October. It is best in the sun but appears to have no soil preferences. Never growing much above 3ft with a slightly spreading habit, it fits in well wherever it is placed.

Away from the garden to a most lovely house plant, *Streptocarpus* Constant Nymph; it well deserved the first-class certificate it received at the 1965 Chelsea Flower Show. The flowers are not unlike a flattish foxglove, a deep violet in colour and most graceful. One of its great virtues is that it flourishes no matter what type of

heating is used, and it stands up to quite long periods of dryness—
a serious consideration for anyone who is often away from home.

THE FRAGRANT HERB   Mary Crosse

Of recent years I have been watching with interest a non-flowering
chamomile grown by Dorothy Sewart at Lower Treneague near
Wadebridge (see pictures on page 123). Some thirty years ago
she bought an eighteenth-century stone-built cottage in a lovely
stretch of Cornish countryside. Today it is surrounded by a nature
reserve of nine acres under the control of the Cornwall Naturalists'
Trust, on whose behalf she acts as warden. She made a charming
wild garden amid the boulders and streams of the valley; and she
stocked the garden round the house with rare and unusual plants,
many from cuttings given to her from other Cornish gardens.
Among them was a single cutting of *Anthemis nobilis* which she
planted in a crevice among blue-slate paving-stones. There to her
surprise, instead of sending up a straggling stalk and producing a
flowerhead, this chamomile developed a spreading prostrate
growth without sign of flowering. The following spring one of the
paving-stones was replaced with soil, in which the chamomile was
replanted after being split up. Gradually more stones were removed to accommodate what was becoming a little chamomile
lawn; throughout this period there was still no sign of a flower.

Inquiries revealed that the original stock probably came from
one of the Buckingham Palace lawns of *A nobilis*; but they are
mown weekly to remove flower-heads and to keep the sward short.
This increased the mystery of the lack of flowers at Treneague and,
on the advice of the county horticultural consultant, a specimen was
sent to Wisley for identification. One of the Royal Horticultural
Society's botanists told Dorothy Sewart that she had probably
been extremely fortunate in having produced a clone of the species
which never, or but rarely, flowers. During tests at Wisley no
blooms appeared.

Meanwhile the little lawn in front of the Cornish cottage had
developed into a close sward of a lovely green, from which there

was a delightful fragrance, especially after rain. It was found to be hard-wearing and, summer and winter alike, retained its colour and was very resilient when trodden. It also did not appear to harbour insects. Over and above all these advantages, it was found to maintain its low growth without cutting. So Dorothy Sewart realised that she might cultivate her chamomile on an extensive scale and market it. Now, under the cultivar name of *Chamaemelum nobile* Treneague, it is for sale and evoking much interest. I saw the plant being tested in Pennsylvania last year and was told that it showed promise of doing well there too.

This chamomile is extremely easy to grow. A hundred shoots, planted firmly 5 or 6in apart, are required per 3 sq yds. Each, if growing happily, will form a prostrate mass of 8 to 10 sq in in one season. While the sward is developing, the ground must be kept clear of weeds; and in the autumn it should be given a top dressing of compost, soil, gravel or leaf-mould. Its growth, especially in lime-free soil, is amazing. Once developed, the sward requires neither weeding, cutting nor rolling. Planting in shade is not recommended, as it will then require clipping occasionally. At Lower Treneague it is used also as a weed-smotherer, as ground cover in difficult spots such as most gardens possess, as a plant for crazy paving and also for paths. I would like to cut a seat in a bank and plant it with this fragrant herb, thus emulating Thomas Hyll who, in 1577, wrote in the *Gardener's Labyrinth* of using it for 'benches to sytte on'. In the days of the first Elizabeth chamomile lawns were frequently grown. With the arrival of *Chamaemelum nobile* Treneague history may well repeat itself.

FLOWERS, FRUIT AND FRAGRANCE
David C. Dallimore

It is dangerous to enthuse about a particular plant, for tastes differ so much that you can easily land yourself in trouble. When I recommended *Viburnum rhytidophyllum*, a firm favourite of mine, the recipient thought it hideous. But with the elaeagnuses I feel safer, because among the various deciduous and evergreen species there are excellent variegated forms, edible fruit and scented flowers in late autumn. As a genus they are neglected. In how many lists of autumn-flowering shrubs, for example, are they mentioned? Yet they will grow in any type of soil with little attention, preferably in full sun, though the evergreen species are shade-tolerant and wind-resistant.

The origin of the name oleaster seems rather obscure and, whereas in the past it was used for the whole genus, it now generally refers only to *Elaeagnus angustifolia*. A native of southeast Europe, where it is known as Jerusalem willow, this is a strong-growing deciduous shrub with long narrow leaves, white underneath and grey-green above. The young shoots are also white, so the plant has a somewhat ghostly appearance. It is certainly willow-like, though easily distinguished by the typical small fragrant yellow flowers in June and the silvery-grey edible fruits which follow. It is excellent for grey foliage schemes, and I consider it superior to the willow-leafed pear, *Pyrus salicifolia*. *E umbellata* is similar in growth but has larger leaves which are bright on the upper surface. It is most spectacular when carrying its usually heavy crop of silver-speckled red berries. Most noted for its fruit is *E multiflora* (or *edulis*), with similar leaf colouring. In summer it bears a profusion of long-stalked orange fruits which are juicy and have a pleasant, if rather pungent, taste. In France, I believe, they are used for making a preserve. For those who like testing and tasting the unusual this shrub is worth planting. It will grow to about 6ft and has scented cream flowers in spring.

These three are easy vigorous shrubs. The other deciduous species, *E commutata* (or *argentea*), is unfortunately less obliging. In its native North America it is said to attain 10ft, but in Britain it is usually a slow-growing, rather puny plant with the appearance of the weakling in the litter. This is a pity because the silver berry has the most startling colouring of all. Again rather willow-like, the leaves are much smaller, intensely silver all over, and spring from young shoots which appear to have been sprayed with bronze metallic paint. The combination of stem and leaf is delightful, especially as the bronze spreads slightly into the silver, as if the spraying had been carelessly done.

Of the evergreen species, *E macrophylla* from China and Japan grows strongly up to 10ft and has the largest leaves of the genus—4in long and nearly as wide. At first they are silver on both sides; but the upper surface rapidly changes to grey-green, and the underside becomes intensely silver. As a foliage plant it deserves wider recognition, being particularly striking when the leaves are turned by the wind. Bright red fruits follow the scented flowers in autumn. Also autumn-flowering is *E glabra* but, whereas *E macrophylla* makes a wide spreading bush, this is a rampant grower which will scramble 15ft through a tree, given the chance. The leaves are equally long, but narrower and bright green on the upper surface. Underneath they have the typical silver lustre but are spotted with bronze scales which radiate from the leaf-stalks.

E pungens and its varieties are the most widely planted of the genus, though by no means the earliest to be cultivated. They possess attractive and varied foliage; but they rarely produce fruit, and so lack one of the great charms of other species. All have leathery leaves, silver on the underside, rust-brown young shoots and scented flowers in autumn. The type plant is a dense shrub with distinctive wavy-edged leaves. In favourable conditions it will reach 15ft. *E p variegata* has bright green leaves with a narrow marginal band of pale cream, but pride of place goes to *E p maculata* (or *aureo-variegata*) which is without doubt in the top rank. The variegation here consists of a broad central zone of bright clear yellow bordered by a margin of dark green; between them are areas of colour midway between the two. The most fascinating characteristic to me is that each zone is clearly defined and distinct from its neighbour, so that the upper surface is three-coloured.

The evergreen varieties are sometimes grafted on to seedling stocks of the free-berrying species and produce suckers. These should be removed as they appear. Otherwise no regular pruning is required, beyond that necessary to form a well-balanced plant.

WHEN TO PRUNE FLOWERING SHRUBS
A. W. J. Young

As autumn approaches, dead flower-spikes and straggling seasonal growth can make the shrub garden look ragged and neglected; but the temptation to wade in with shears and secateurs must be resisted. A little judicious pruning will be beneficial, and dead flower-heads can be cut off with advantage. Anything more is best left till the spring as, with few exceptions, heavy cutting at this time of year will certainly reduce and may even prevent flowering next spring and summer.

The basic reasons for pruning flowering shrubs are the same as for fruit trees: to control shape and improve the quality of bloom and berry. Light pruning increases the quantity of bloom but can lead to loss of quality; in older bushes it results in little or no fresh growth. Heavy cutting leads to vigorous growth, often at the expense of flower production; but several shrubs carry finer flowers and will remain vigorous for longer if some or all of the older wood is removed annually. The appropriate time for this will depend on the month of flowering and whether the blooms are borne on the current season's growth or that of the previous year.

Most spring-flowering shrubs come into the latter category and are best pruned by cutting back the flowered shoot to a strong new bud immediately after flowering. Forsythias treated in this way will produce strong new growths during the summer and be covered with large trusses of perfect blooms the following spring; and witch-hazel, chaenomeles (japonica), wintersweet, *Lonicera purpusii* and flowering currants will all benefit from judicious thinning of older branches as soon as they have flowered.

Forsythias and chaenomeles growing as hedges or against walls respond well to spur pruning of the current year's growth. Rambler roses produce their best display on vigorous shoots of the previous season, and most or all of the older wood can be cut out each year immediately after flowering or in the early autumn.

The outstanding example of a shrub that flowers best on young shoots of the current year's growth is *Buddleia davidi*—not to be confused with *B globosa*, which bears its flower-heads on older wood and requires only light pruning after flowering. The flowered shoots should be cut back to within 12in of the main framework in the autumn or, especially in districts where hard February frost can be expected, in March.

The deciduous varieties of ceanothus, the dogwoods, *Hydrangea paniculata*, hypericums, outdoor fuchsias, *Tamarix pentandra* and, of course, hybrid tea and floribunda roses will also give more brilliant displays if cut back hard to within two or three buds of the main branches as soon as the danger of severe frost has passed. Clearly, therefore, most of the pruning of flowering shrubs should be carried out in the spring and not during the late summer and autumn.

Climbing hybrid tea, as distinct from rambler, roses are best pruned in the spring, care then being taken to preserve most of the older wood and merely spur back the previous year's flowering shoots to within one or two buds of the main framework. If these roses are cut back to ground level they are liable to lose their climbing characteristic; but they will make excellent informal shrubs if all strong growths are cut back to 5–6ft and allowed to branch out freely.

Evergreens require little or no attention; where cutting back is required, as for evergreen hedges, it is best carried out in May when all danger of frost is over. Some evergreens are better left alone, because they resent hard pruning; but box, laurel, lonicera (*nitida*), privet and rhododendron are exceptions to the rule. They may be cut right back and completely rejuvenated when they become straggling or overgrown. Yew and holly hedges may also be pruned hard, provided that the work is spread over three years, one side being cut back each year.

Hedges of *Berberis darwinii*, *B stenophylla*, escallonia and lavender can be cut back after flowering to ensure a fresh supply of vigorous flowering branches for the ensuing year. In addition, some shortening of long shoots of replanted evergreens is beneficial and should be done at the time of planting, in the early autumn. Brooms will die if cut back into older wood, but the trimming of green shoots after flowering will help to lessen the tendency of these plants to make straggling growth.

Although older bushes of lilac and hydrangea will benefit from a certain amount of thinning, which is best done after flowering, remember that next year's flowers are produced in the terminal buds of young shoots and from the buds developing immediately below the flower-head, so pruning will reduce the number of new flower-heads. But the size and quality of those left will be improved, and a reduction in the number of flowering shoots is desirable, particularly with the garden varieties of hydrangea. Apart from this only the dead flower-heads should be removed.

Branches of variegated trees and shrubs will occasionally revert to green. The offending branch should then be removed as soon as possible by cutting it right back to its junction with the main framework. Unwanted branches of all species of shrub, such as strong shoots growing into neighbouring bushes, should also be cut right out. Indeed trimming back is useless, and garden shears should be kept for tidying hedges. Secateurs, knife or pruning saw are the tools for the shrub garden. The same principle should be applied to flowering trees: once the main framework is established, they normally require only occasional thinning by the removal of complete branches during the dormant season.

Many lovely flowering shrubs have not been mentioned in this brief survey, as they require little or no pruning beyond the periodical removal of dead and diseased wood, coupled with judicious thinning of overcrowded branches. Japanese maples, azaleas, camellias, choisya, cotoneasters, daphnes, magnolias, shrubby potentillas, pyracanthas, skimmias and most species of viburnum belong to this group, and also the coniferous evergreens. As with fruit trees the rule, when in doubt, is to leave well alone.

SQUITCH GRASS

> Touch me not!
> For merry-begot
> Seed of wizard
> And wrangling witch,
> I'll bake and burn
> And still return
> To stick in your gizzard
> And choke your ditch.
> Signed—Squitch.

Anne Johnson

COMMON WHEAT GRASS John Blackwood

'Its roots are most difficult of extirpation, and will retain their vitality amid many injuries.' So wrote Anne Pratt of couch grass in her *British Grasses and Sedges* in the 1860s. In September of last year an officer of the Weed Research Organisation was still obliged to admit that it is a menace in spite of chemical control methods; that it can reduce yields and interfere with harvesting. In the last hundred years farmers have cleared our cornfields of yellow charlock, orange marigold and scarlet poppy, so that acres of down and wold have become endless sheets of green from April to July. The grasses, on the other hand, especially the bents, black grass, wild oats and couch, have resisted the weedkillers quite well. Since they are green, like the crops among which they live, they are not obvious until their flower-heads show above the ears of corn.

The flower-heads of couch appear above the crop in August. They are not branched panicles, like those of the bents or wild oats, but spikes like those of wheat; the spikelets, each consisting of several small flowers or florets, are fixed directly to the flower stalk or rachis. Linnaeus put couch with the bread wheats in the genus *Triticum*, and English writers on botany and agriculture called it common wheat grass. A glance at an ear of couch alongside one of a new bread wheat, such as Maris Widgeon, shows that even to-day the early writers could be justified. Two hundred years ago, before we had improved wheat, the ear was, to use the breeder's terminology, much more lax and less dense than it is today; so the ears of the two plants appeared much alike.

Ears of couch and of modern wheat

About 1812 the botanists transferred couch to the genus *Agropyron*, and today they call it *A repens*. Unlike wheat, couch is perennial, has underground stems or rhizomes and often fails to

set seed. I have heard farmers say that couch does not set seed; and one year I collected, from a wide area, spikes from which I obtained only a few grains, none of which germinated. Others have obtained similar results. Couch is self-sterile, so plants from one rhizome will not set seed unless they receive pollen from one of a different stock—a rather more common occurrence than is sometimes thought.

If couch is weak in seed setting, it makes up for this many times over with its power-packed rhizomes. I have cut these into half-inch pieces and found that, while none completely devoid of buds will grow, those with only one bud will shoot up from a depth of 3in. Others have found that twin-budded pieces have penetrated the surface from 32in down; and single-bud fragments of only 0.15in long have grown from a depth of 4in. Reproduction from seed is always chancy, and couch has gained by being able to spread from a piece of itself little larger than a seed. The rhizomes have sharp hardened tips which help them to penetrate the soil.

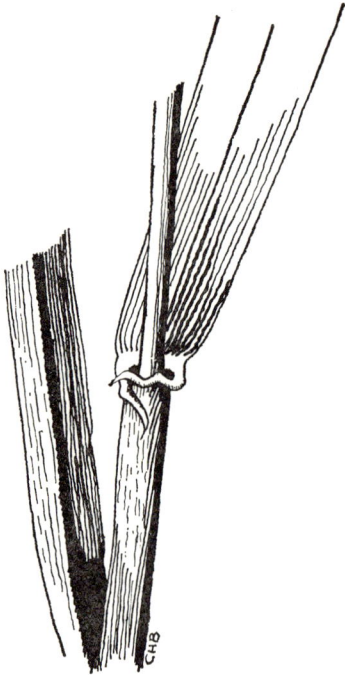

Auricle of couch grass

If it is a commonplace of horticultural advice that you must remove every fraction of an inch of this weed, how can you recognise it without rhizome or flower-head before you start to dig? Margaret Plues wrote in her *British Grasses* (1867): 'Leaves turning to one side give the grass a marked appearance and make it easy of recognition.' This feature certainly helps when there are clumps among barley tillers, but it seems optimistic to try to use it in the tangle of a garden. More helpful characteristics are the flatness of the leaf blade, due to the absence of a prominent mid rib, and its relative width in the centre. Unlike most grasses, the blade of couch tapers towards both the apex and the place where it joins the sheath or rounded part of the leaf. The point where the blade joins the sheath provides the most certain means of identifying the plant by its visible parts. Here a shallow fleshy collar or ligule sticks out to form two minute ears or auricles, finer than those of barley, meadow fescue or Italian rye-grass, for which you are unlikely to mistake couch anyway. In the picturesque words of H. Marshall Ward in *Grasses* (1901), these 'horizontal shelves, like a Byron collar' wrap 'round the sides of the throat of the sheath.' The auricles are visible to the naked eye.

'It is frequent in neglected gardens and richly cultivated soil,' wrote the Scots doctor Richard Parnell in one of the earliest authoritative books on the *Grasses of Britain* (1845). 'Under every rotation of crops with the best management possible, couch accumulates in all soils' was the verdict of George Sinclair in his famous nineteenth-century treatise on weeds and grasses, *Hortus Gramineus Woburnensis*. Can any good be

Couch rhizome

said for a plant which so outrageously mocks and defies us? Margaret Plues claimed that it was 'good food for pigs, and in time of famine' could be made into bread, but added with true Victorian caution that 'food both for man and beast is too easy to get to render it worth while to spend labour in getting couch-grass roots for edible purposes.'

Many authors point out that couch is eaten, as is often observed,

by cats and dogs as an emetic. The nineteenth-century German botanist Eduard Hackel extracts, as it were, the last ounce of goodness from it: 'The juicy runners and rhizomes are nourishing for cattle; they contain 3 per cent sugar and 6–8 per cent triticin, a gummy carbohydrate, and are officially known as *Radix graminis*. The extract acts as a solvent upon collections of the mucous membranes, and in infections of the intestinal canal. A syrup and even an alcohol are made from it.' The Germans appear to have taken their serious scientist at his word, for in the 1914–18 war they were said to have fed on the carbohydrate.

One gardener wrote: 'To touch it is unpleasant. It has got a nasty roughness to it. Docks have spots, but you never see anything wrong with couch.' Couch appears indeed to suffer from no disease, and it is tempting to wish upon it something powerful enough (like myxomatosis) to 'extirpate' it. On the other hand we may hesitate to deny the right to live to any created thing, even if its ideal habitat is our cultivated land. There is also the chance that a disease of couch might attack fodder grasses and even wheat. It is in the same tribe as wheat, and scientists have crossed it with wheat to try to make use of its disease-resisting properties. If you have seen one of the finest examples of the plant breeder's skill, a modern high-yielding wheat, blood-red with rust, you will probably be in favour of keeping couch in existence for a while.

THE STRAWBERRY BARREL   Raymond Bush

If you are pushed for space you can have a strawberry patch in a barrel. Being a woodland plant, the strawberry does not mind shade so long as it gets a reasonable amount of daylight. A forty-gallon barrel is needed, and if it is to last well it should be of oak with hoops in sound condition.

First bore in the bottom four ¾in holes for drainage. Then turn the barrel on its side and along a line chalked round the centre bore six evenly spaced holes. With the barrel still on its side, chalk a line on each side of the centre one, half way between it and the top and bottom, and bore eight holes along each, making sure that the new holes fall between those on the centre line. Then give the hoops two coats of paint; if they are rusty, clean them off well with a wire brush beforehand. Oak needs no paint, and be sure not to use creosote which will kill any plant it touches.

Next prepare a really rich soil mixture: old manure chopped very fine, leaf-mould and old turf or sandy loam can be used in equal proportions if the first two are really well rotted. Put in the bottom of the barrel a 4in layer of broken brick and rubble or gravel, and over it form a central drainage channel by rolling a piece of stiff cardboard into a tube at least 4in across, tying it in position with one end on the rubble and filling it with similar materials. Add enough of the soil to reach the first line of holes and press it down. If you have some moss, place a wisp round the neck of each runner to keep it central in its hole and to prevent the soil coming out.

Having inserted runners in the bottom line of holes all round the barrel, add more soil, taking care to spread the roots as well as you can so that they do not all lie on the same plane. When you reach the central line of holes you can pull up and refill the cardboard tube, replacing it before you insert more plants and continue to add soil until the top line is reached. Once the holes in this are filled, the central drainage channel can be stopped, the tube taken away and the barrel topped up with soil. Ordinarily it should be watered through a rose from the top, but while the plants are getting established an occasional syringe-full of water can be forced in round each.

If you plant the barrel before the end of September you will be able to pick fruit next summer.

BACTERIAL BONFIRE   Lawrence D. Hills

The difference between a good compost heap and rechristened rubbish heap lies mainly in the 'activator'—the paper and sticks to light the bacterial bonfire that should cook weed seeds like grains of rice, leaving behind rich humus and balanced plant foods instead of quickly spent ashes. We need never supply bacteria, which are everywhere; but they must have nitrogen to make up the proteins of their bodies. They can then multiply in our garden rubbish as fast as they do in lawn-mowings, which they can heat within a few hours to a temperature too hot for the hand to bear. The activator should contain nitrogen and also calcium, because lawn-mowings in particular may make a heap so acid that several especially useful bacteria die out for lack of lime enough to keep the heap near-neutral. Lawn-mowings alone soon stop heating and become a slimy mass that stays unchanged, because they bind together and exclude the air. The 'fire' then dies for lack of oxygen, and bad silage results in place of compost. So a good air supply from below is the second most important requirement for a compost heap.

Heaps made in the open do not decay on the outsides, which cannot reach the 120 to 160° F that must be achieved all through to make sure of killing the spores of all plant diseases and weed seeds. They must be turned to bring them sides to middle, and

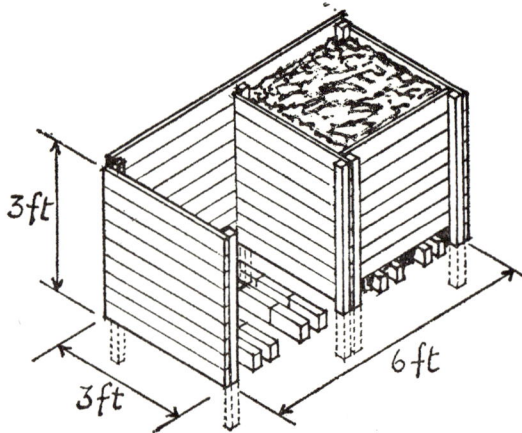

'New Zealand' compost box

they rarely heat as well as heaps made in what is called a 'New Zealand box'—the best and tidiest method for small gardens.

An E-shaped box with two compartments, one full and the other filling, each 3ft square and high, takes about 250ft of ½in by 4in sawn planks and seven 4ft lengths of 2in by 2in timber. Saw up the planks into twelve 6ft lengths for the back, thirty-six 3ft for sides and middle, and twenty-two 2ft 11in for the removable loose board fronts. Then paint all the wood, especially the sawn ends, with Solignum or Cuprinol, not creosote.

When the wood is dry, lay the three uprights for the back a yard apart on flat ground and nail the 6ft planks across them, leaving 1ft of each post sticking out at the bottom. Then nail twelve 3ft pieces at one end to each of three 2in by 2in posts. Dig six holes to take the uprights. Insert the three for the back first and ram the soil firmly round them; then put in the front posts, nailing the free ends of the boards to the back ones. The spare 4ft post should be nailed against the centre post in the middle of the 'E', to hold the shorter planks for the loose front.

There are eleven, not twelve, of these for each compartment, as two double rows of bricks placed about 2in apart from back to front, with 2ft between the pairs, stick out under the bottom board, which rests across them. These boards, like the others, are held in place by the material behind them. On top of the bricks put about 2in of stemmy rubbish to prevent weeds and mowings from blocking the essential air channel. Add 8in of material, including domestic wastes in the middle, and then scatter about 2oz lime per sq yd of layer. Pile on another 8in of weeds, shaking off as much soil as possible, because no heap has heat enough to cook weed seeds and couch-grass roots inside lumps of cold clay. On this spread about two forkfuls of any available animal manure: poultry (even from batteries), rabbit and pigeon manure are extra good. Add more rubbish, then lime again, and so on like a giant layer-cake.

There are many variations on this theme. Those who have wood or peat fires can replace lime with wood ashes, to use their calcium and add their potash. The manure layers can be increased to 1in in thickness to use up pigeon manure, which is too strong to be applied direct in the garden and is often obtainable free for the fetching. Many composters live in towns, where manure is scarce, costly and bad, and for them there are several proprietary activators. These should be used sparingly as the makers recommend; it is important to remember that you are feeding not pigs, but bacteria.

An excellent and cheap activator is a mixture of one part of dried seaweed manure to three of dried sludge from any far-sighted council. The sludge will contain lime, so only one kind of layer is needed, and the two together heat far better than either separately. This mixture is recommended for those who have trouble in getting heaps to heat. Winter heaps will need a corrugated-iron or polythene cover to prevent rain washing away plant foods, and summer ones should be watered in drought.

NO DIG

When Father Adam and his peccant mate,
Stunned by the clanging of the garden gate,
Strove to recall the details of the curse,
They wondered whether by some imp perverse
They had misheard
A word.

Dig. What that word to Adam now conveyed!
(He was the first that called a spade a spade.)
For him and for his progeny it spelt
The toil, the sweat, the blister and the welt,
And for his back
The rack.

Though memories dimmed, yet he could not recall
That digging was required before the Fall.
In that fair garden all things seemed to grow
Without the need of spade or fork or hoe.
One did not dig
The fig.

The memories die. The strange obsession stays
And plagues the soul of Adam all his days,
And as he passes to his doubtful rest
He leaves his tainted offspring, too, obsessed
To grasp the helve
And delve.

So man, self-damned, condemned himself to use
The tools that Mother Nature would refuse,
And bring with unremitting toil to birth
His scanty substance from the tortured earth.
Why labour so
To grow?

But now has dawned a more enlightened day:
The 'Ploughman's Folly' passes on its way.
Now ended is the wily serpent's term;
His doom is lifted by the humbler worm
Who can reverse
The curse.

F. B. Julian

THE EVER-GAY WINDOW-SILL — Coryla Grafton

There is not much money for luxuries on a chalky Chiltern farm, but I was determined that my sitting-room window-sill should always be gay with flowers. Fortunately the window was large and faced due south. I nailed a board along the ledge, painted it green and placed there two *Primula obconica* presented to me because they gave their owner a rash; one of these plants lasted seven years in almost continuous bloom. For the summer I had begonias, but during the war I lost them and had to make do with geraniums. When begonia tubers came on the market again I treated myself to six from a good strain and started them in March in a box on the kitchen shelf. They have brightened the window-sill from June till mid-October every year since.

One spring I bought a small *Primula malacoides* from the postman for sixpence. After it had finished flowering I left it outside for the seeds to ripen; then I scattered these in two seed boxes painted green. In the autumn when I brought the boxes indoors they were full of seedlings which made a perfect window decoration—a miniature mauve forest—from January till April. The pelargoniums are then ready; those lovely old-fashioned flowers that are now not nearly so widely grown as they deserve. I begged a cutting of a charming pink one from a cottage window in exchange for a *Primula malacoides*, and it has grown and multiplied exceedingly.

When a cyclamen I had been given achieved a seed pod I planted the seeds in a pan and kept them at the end of the window-sill through the winter, potting them up in the spring and standing them outside in some ashes. At the beginning of October they were in bud, ready to come indoors to replace the begonias. For eighteen years I have managed to have an unbroken succession of colour—not without protest from the farmer, who dislikes having his view obscured.

POT-POURRI   Marion Henderson

The making of sweet-scented pot-pourri was one of the accomplishments of Victorian women. I remember the large untidy herb-patch, near the apple trees and straw bee-skeps, where my grandmother grew mint, thyme, lavender and rosemary. Like others of her generation, she valued flowers more for their scent than for their colour. The scent of a plant, she believed, added greatly to its beauty and 'stirred the mind more deeply than seeing or hearing'. Even church-going was not complete without a sprig of lad's love wrapped in her handkerchief to regale her during the long sermon. Her clothing always smelt of lavender, for she used to stitch sachets of it into the lining of her tightly buttoned bodice, and the old house had the same sweet smell, especially the great bedroom and the four-poster with its lavender-scented sheets.

Although grandmother knew the recipe for pot-pourri by heart, she invariably consulted Culpeper's herbal every time she filled with her fragrant mixture the old blue bowl which stood beside the precious family album on a highly polished table in the middle of the parlour. Small holes in the lid allowed the scents to penetrate the room.

Our visits used to coincide with the making of pot-pourri, some time between July and September. As children we were simply asked to go out into the garden and gather some of the precious ingredients. We picked roses—second blooms of the red damask beauties, the perfume of which surpassed everything else in the garden—shredded the petals, and left them on a large tray to dry in the sun. We added tiny leaves of sweet briar, a few bits of fragrant mignonette from the herb-patch and scarlet clove carnations. We rubbed handfuls of pale purple lavender flowers to get them to the right size, and took a leaf or two of bay and a few of rosemary, thyme, sage and balm, which we mixed all together.

It was at this stage that grandmother herself took complete charge. Today we know the ingredients she added: two level cupfuls of salt, a good pinch of cloves, the same of musk, half a cupful of powdered orris root, the same of ginger, nutmeg, the cut-up rind of a lemon that had been left to dry and a cupful of finely shredded and dried mint. She mixed these well and added alternate layers of flowers, stirring occasionally, until the willow-pattern bowl was filled to the top. Then she pressed the mixture down and chose delphiniums from the second flowering to give it her favourite touch of blue.

It was a delight to take off the lid of the blue bowl, and try to sort out the different scents. Some, like thyme and verbena, were lemony; others, like the clove carnation, sweet and spicy. And we could always recognise the sweet stale smell of musk and roses.

A LILY FOR BEGINNERS Geoffrey Vevers

It was my old friend V.M.H. who started me off growing lilies. In 1948, about Christmas time, he sent me some seed of *Lilium philippinense* from his own wonderful garden in the Cotswolds. I did not know much about growing anything then, but on 4 January I sowed the seed hopefully in a pan of ordinary garden soil put through a sieve (see pictures on page 124). Forty-eight days later the seedlings came up just like onions—slender green staples which after a few days straightened out into something that looked like blades of grass, only round. They grew beautifully for about a month; then one by one they flagged and I found that they were being eaten off at the roots by very small but vicious larvae which had hatched out in the soil. I saved only one seedling out of about fifty. This I put in a thumb pot of fresh soil and wrote to V.M.H. for more seed. It came by return of post.

By this time I had been introduced to the marvels of John Innes seed compost, and here, to those who do not know them or are wavering, let me say that all the JI composts are more than worth the money they cost, but see that you get them from someone who specialises in them. The second lot of seedlings came just like the first, only much more quickly, and this time they did not get mown down by any subterranean bug. There seem to be two schools of thought about whether one should prick out lily seedlings or let them grow on in the seed pan. My feeling is that quickly maturing lilies like *L philippinense* should be pricked out into a stronger compost early on, but that slow-growing lilies like *L auratum* should be left in the original pan and moved later.

When my ewe lamb from the first batch outgrew its thumb pot I transferred it to a long-tom pot with some peat mixed with well-rotted cow-manure in the bottom over the crocks, then a layer of JI potting compost No 1. The bulb was now about an inch in diameter and had good roots. I was careful not to let these come in contact with the dung, and covered the whole completely with the compost, keeping the bulb well down in the pot, because *L philippinense* is a stem-rooter. When I saw it had got root in the new pot and was obviously flourishing, I put it outside and tried to forget about it, but I could not, because after all it was my ewe lamb, so I looked at it most days and occasionally watered it. It continued to flourish and threw up a strong shoot and a lovely fat bud which opened with a flourish of a 6in long trumpet on 1 June, eighteen months after the seed was sown.

That was not the end of the story. I brought the lily into the house and put it on a sunny window-sill, where for three weeks it continued to bloom and smell deliciously. As soon as the pollen was dry I cut off an anther and rubbed it on the tip of the stigma, which by that time was ready to be fertilised; I had no other lily for cross-pollination. When the flower faded I put my now rather bedraggled lamb on the steps of the veranda. A seed pod soon formed, and as the weather became cold and wet I brought it back into a spare room to ripen. This took a long time, but one sunny day I found the table on which it stood covered with seeds, nearly all with the brown patch in the centre denoting fertility. I put them in the linen cupboard for the night and sowed half of them a day or two later, with the result that I had a pan of dozens of *L philip-pinese* seedlings two years almost to the day after sowing the original seed.

The seed pod of this lily is a beautiful and wonderful thing, about $3\frac{1}{2}$in long and, when closed, about $\frac{3}{4}$in across. It has the appearance of being divided longitudinally into six parts, but when it is ripe only three of the divisions split, the remaining ones being the attachments of the three internal sections into which it is divided. When it starts to dry it opens gradually from the top, and the flat triangular seeds that lie one above the other all the way down begin to dry from the top. In order to stop the pod from opening too quickly and releasing unripe seeds from below, a wonderful mechanism has been evolved. Between each of the sections is what might be described as a lattice window, rather Gothic in shape, formed by the stretching of slender filaments of fibre from the edge of each of the three main divisions. Although the filaments are very fine, they must be strong, because they have to overcome a certain amount of tension caused by the shrinking of the pod as it dries. The 'windows' are doubtless for the purpose of allowing ventilation of the seeds throughout the pod, so that there is even ripening. If by any chance, owing to inclement weather, the pod does not ripen fairly quickly and the side 'windows' remain shut, the seed may turn colour but will invariably be damp and mouldy and completely infertile.

When the second batch of seedlings were large enough to handle I planted them outside in a shady spot in a mixture of loam, peat and cow-manure. Some of the stronger ones flowered in September, but although they set seed it was not fertile, as the autumn of 1950 was cold and wet. However, my crowning triumph was yet to come. That autumn I visited V.M.H. and told him of my success and of the supply of seed I had collected from my ewe lamb. 'Can you let me have some?' he said. 'All my *philippinense* failed to set seed this season.'

THE ROCKERY BED   Elizabeth Cross

Some gardens have difficult spots, places where a splash of colour is needed, but which either become waterlogged or dry out in summer. There may be costly professional ways of curing these defects, but why not rockery beds? Mine has been a great success, and it was simply made. You empty the bed of old plants, dig in all the compost, manure, peat or leaf-mould you can spare and, as a long-term investment, add a generous sprinkling of bone meal. Then collect rough stones (the bigger the better), old weathered bricks and broken flowerpots, and half bury them to form an irregular series of mounds and pockets. One or two large pieces of old paving are a help, but it is quite possible to build a rockery bed with middle-sized stones. The aim is to form drainage spaces for wet weather, and damp spots for plant roots in the summer.

I planted my first rockery bed with a mixture that would give colour and interest almost the year round. Near daffodils and dwarf tulips I put primula Wanda and the ordinary yellow primrose. I planted a few roots of large-flowering michaelmas daisies and nasturtiums, and here and there old-fashioned verbena provides a cloud of green and a most delicious perfume.

This is no bed for a man or a professional gardener who loves to dig thoroughly and replant properly. Here it is a matter of going on your knees with a hand fork, a bucket and sometimes a trowel—a peaceful, pottering sort of job. Each bed fills itself nicely, but the stones prevent overcrowding or pushing of neighbours. I give my bed occasional sprinklings of lime and bone meal, and sometimes a mulch of compost if there is promise of a very dry spell, but generally I leave it alone. I am sure most plants prefer to be undisturbed once they are comfortable, as mine appear to be in the rockery bed.

THE FIRST MAN TO MAKE A PLANT HYBRID
Sir Daniel Hall, FRS

It is not often that the man of science, as such, finds himself bidden to church. But every year in June a service is held in Shoreditch

Church to which representatives of such bodies as the Ministry of Agriculture, the Royal Society and the Royal Horticultural Society are invited. Thomas Fairchild was a citizen and freeman of London (1667–1729), a gardener, who had his nursery in Shoreditch and left a sum of money, now administered by the Worshipful Company of Gardeners, to provide for an annual discourse on the beneficence of God as exemplified in the plants of our gardens.

But good Thomas Fairchild was more than mindful of his Creator, he was something of a creator himself. He has a niche in botanical and horticultural history as the first man deliberately to make a plant hybrid. Richard Bradley, Professor of Botany in the University of Cambridge, writes in 1719, 'For example, the Carnation and the Sweet William are in some respects alike, the Farina of one will impregnate the other, and the seed so enliven'd will produce a plant differing from either, as may now be seen in the garden of *Mr. Thomas Fairchild of Hoxton*, a plant neither *Sweet William* nor *Carnation*, but resembling both equally, which was raised from the seed of a *Carnation* that had been impregnated by the Farina of the Sweet William.'

This, you will remember, was before any general recognition of the existence of sex in plants, for Camerarius, who was the first to give any demonstration of this fact, had only published his *Epistola de Sexa Plantarum* in 1696, and from other sources we may conclude that his letter to a colleague in Tübingen, was unknown even to scientific men in England. The new hybrid, 'Fairchild's Sweet William,' as it was called, was propagated and held its place in gardens for a long time, indeed only a few years ago one of my colleagues saw a specimen in an experimental garden in New York. Thomas Fairchild's experiment was not immediately followed up; it was not until the nineteenth century that men like Thomas Andrew Knight began to utilise cross fertilisation for the improvement of plants. But Thomas Fairchild was a citizen as well as a gardener; he founded his lecture to help his neighbours.

Shoreditch has lost its gardens; but as the Chaplain of the Gardeners' Company reminded us in his discourse, the love of beauty is inherent in humanity, and the inhabitants of Shoreditch have not lost their delight in flowers. Even the determination to clear its slums arises from this same instinct for beauty and order.

Fame among men hangs but by a slender thread and there are many poorer titles to remembrance than to be associated with a flower or a fruit. Few men's names are in more mouths than Mr Cox of Colnbrook, that retired brewer who more than a hundred years ago gave Cox's Orange Pippin to the world.

This was written in 1935. The service to which the author refers is no longer held.

Ed

THE STORY OF A GARDEN

Three years ago
Newly-married my neighbours came to the new
bungalow.
Hidden by lace
Curtains, their indoor life was their own business,
But I knew them when
They walked in their Adam and Eve aspect of rearing a young
garden.

All was to do:
The raw hillside to dig, the tenured brambles to hack through,
The soil to turn
And sift and lime and rake level, the weeds to burn,
Paths to ram hard,
And tenderly the young fruit trees to be settled in the new
orchard.

And I could hear
Late through the April dusk their voices floating bird-clear;
He steadily
Counting the paced plan of where lawn and plots should be,
And she to him
Retailing her gay gazette of lilac-bud and transplanted lupin.

Now in this third
April the winter trimness of earth and branch is blurred
With imminent
Green thrust from sap and seed well-cared-for and confident;
And Adam goes
Slowly around his garden dressed as a soldier and Eve follows.

In careful and few
Words (for time is short) he counsels her what she must do
As summer comes on.
She nods, and stares at his boots, and promises that all shall
be done.
With babbled cries
Answering back the thrushes, the two-year child trots about
Paradise.

Sylvia Townsend Warner

I am loth to break the spell of this poem, but solicitude for young fruit
trees compels me to add the severely practical note that these should be
settled not tenderly, but firmly.

Ed

FLOWERS OR BIRDS?   Lady Janet Bailey

Horticulture is a plaguey enough science in itself without trying to
combine it with aviculture; yet, this is precisely what we have done
in our Wiltshire garden. When first we came to live in the Avon
Valley, we set out lightheartedly to link the two. The lawn at the
back of the house slopes down to a small stream, which at that time
was separated from the main river by a rough meadow island,
elbow-deep in nettles. We, two partners-in-inexperience, cried, the
one, 'Here shall be a water garden!' the other, 'What a place for a
bird sanctuary!'

We knew nothing of the fogs and frosts (early and late) that
infest a river valley, nor of what that gentle river is capable in flood
time. We had yet to learn of the weed-like invasive propensities of
some of the water-loving plants, and to find that it is far easier to
plan a garden within a restricted space than one whose only

boundaries are flat meandering streams. We began operations at the narrowest and least shaggy part of the meadow island, leading two streams across it, to the main river, over miniature waterfalls—is one ever too old to enjoy making a waterfall? While we were planting the sides of these rivulets with forget-me-nots, primulas, astilbes and irises, we enclosed the farther meadow with a wire fence, and therein turned loose a large white sow and her eight young. By the spring, there remained no visible grass, no nettles and no docks. We seeded the well-turned soil, and long before summer we were admiring a velvety lawn. (We were never to admire it again!) Having planted two herbaceous borders, some clumps of poplars, willows and bamboos, we thought our work done; there remained only to erect a fox-and-rat-proof fence for the birds—European, Asiatic, Mongolian and Antipodean— which began to arrive from dealers. A good many birds died on arrival, and some flew away—among them a flamingo; but the majority settled down to destroy the newly-created garden.

The breeds which prefer nesting above ground are supplied with barrels placed in the branches of ancient apple trees and willow trees, and approached by little ladders. It is amusing in springtime to watch the ducks house-hunting. Madam goes up a ladder, inspects a barrel, and returns to report to her lord; then the drake makes his investigation; further and very animated conversation follows before the pair set off to look at the next desirable residence. In spite of all this forethought on our part, some of the birds prefer to select a nesting site for themselves in the herbaceous borders, and no lupin or delphinium ever looks its best after a duck has raised a large family in its bosom. The lupins took their revenge on a pair of spur-winged geese, which died of eating their seeds. The next flowers to suffer were tulips, a pair of cranes being responsible.

Cranes veil a sportive and amorous disposition under a cloak of extreme dignity. During the mating season they dance. With us the long grass walk between the two borders was the stage selected for their *pas-de-deux*, and nothing prettier can be imagined than their poising, stepping and pirouetting. They would *chasse*, and stoop and pick a tulip from the ground, bulb and all, flinging it lightly into the air. Before their courtship days were over, the borders were denuded of every bloom. Aesthetically satisfying as was this display, we felt it was hardly worth the cost of expensive bulbs.

We tried edging the borders with pink and white daisies, but the peacock found the bright starry faces so much to his taste that we decided to give up any form of spring bedding, and have contented ourselves with groupings of polyantha roses, delphiniums, spireas and phloxes, whose vigorous growths are fairly bird-resistant. Turf, alas, is not. Webbed feet are unequalled as weed distributors.

At the far end of the island, where the old cottage stands, we had no sooner planted than we felt a need for some decorative fish—justified by the plea that they would eat the midges. So there came a dozen two-tailed carp and other rare species. For a day we enjoyed the sight of these exotic beauties darting about among the flat-leafed lilies; the next day they were invisible. 'It is hot,' said one of us; 'they are probably sheltering under the leaves.' But when the leaves were raised, only one or two fish emerged. 'Perhaps they are hiding in the mud at the bottom.' Later, from a window we espied an eider-duck sitting on the edge of the pool, fishing. It must have been the last of the consignment that we saw being swallowed.

With the passage of years, the birds have increased in number. Most of the original stock were pinioned, but the greater part of their progeny are free-winged and fly in and out of the enclosure; those who nest without bring their broods back on foot to be admitted into the sanctuary. Today there are in fact two sanctuaries, for part of a stream, a paddock and a small wood in another part of the grounds have been enclosed for the larger birds; here the geese and cranes keep company with gay-plumaged pheasants, peacocks and four delightful wallabys. These are endearing creatures, but we have never decided whether they or the peacocks are responsible for the total disappearance of the daffodils and bluebells we were naturalising in the wood.

WINDFALLS   Arthur P. Jacobs

It was not until our children ran shrieking from the room at the mere mention of apple-pie that Mildred and I decided on other measures to reduce the level of windfalls in the orchard. 'Let's put a basketful outside the front gate each morning, so that people can help themselves,' said Mildred. So we filled a large basket and fixed it in position at dawn. Mildred excitedly kept watch and reported 'Nothing doing' up to the time of my leaving home.

The report was the same when I returned from work in the evening, and we gazed at each other in hurt amazement. Then about seven o'clock two small children knocked gingerly on the door. 'Can we have a pennyworth of windfalls, please?' said the larger, thrusting a couple of halfpennies into Mildred's hand. She smiled and gave the money back. 'You may have all the apples you can carry,' she told them. 'Just help yourselves out of the basket by the gate.' 'But we only want a pennyworth,' one child objected, so Mildred took him gently by the arm and led him to the basket. The children thanked her rather doubtfully, and ten minutes later a sharp bang on the door and a scurry of young feet announced the return of the halfpennies. The apples had hardly been touched.

'It's no good,' said Mildred the following evening. 'Folk just won't help themselves. We must put a notice by the basket pleading with them to take some.' This we did, and after two more blank days we increased the height of the lettering to about a foot; but the apples remained. However, several inquiries as to the price of our windfalls suggested another approach, and our original notice was replaced by a coldly commercial '1d per lb.' A quarter of the basket's contents went immediately, and no one put Mildred to the trouble of weighing up the goods or searching in her purse for change; but after this initial rush, business slackened off. A friend chided us for attempting to undersell the market, so we raised our price to twopence; the following morning at our usual pre-breakfast inspection we found the basket empty and felt dizzy with success. Then, as so often happens, we overdid things. A brazenly chalked '3d' on our notice-board resulted in our losing not only the apples but the basket.

FUNGI GALORE   Stephanie M. Gifford

The time—October; the place—the North Hampshire heathland; the loved one—fungi, in astonishing numbers and variety: for once, contrary to Browning's pessimistic view, they came all together. After an exceptionally wet summer the fungi in and around the small town where I was staying were even more prolific than usual, and the briefest walk into the countryside would produce several kinds new to me. Soon the kitchen table became covered with specimens, gradually disintegrating as I tried to identify them from a pocket guide, partly from a thirst for pure knowledge, partly from a desire to cook anything edible.

Even without going outside the garden it was possible to make an interesting collection. On the lawn, where months earlier mushroom spawn had been planted, a scattered community of deadwhite *Hygrophorus niveus* had appeared, giving a momentary illusion that the planting had been a success. About the same size, but less numerous, was *H ceraceus*, whose cap, stem and gills are all of the same waxy yellow colour and texture. Earlier in the season the lawn had been speckled with *H coccineus*, emerging from the earth to lie in the grass like small cherries, but opening out later to a deep yellow mushroom shape edged with the brilliant red of their youth. Another colourful inhabitant of the October lawn was *Clavaria inaequalis*, one of the 'club' fungi, in shape a spike about an inch and a half high with flattened tip. Deep saffron yellow in colour, an extensive colony of these was reminiscent of a patch of crocus buds.

Tiny delicate 'sunshades', nearly transparent, whose tough stems, like strips of nylon string, betrayed membership of the fairy-ring champignon family, resisted certain identification. There was no doubt, however, about the fairy-rings themselves with their thin wiry stems, alternate long and short gills, and caps that are pale fawn when dry and dark brown when wet. Another characteristic is the circular formation in which they grow: follow the line of the arc made by two or three and you will generally come across several more struggling up through the grass. I fried some fairy-ring champignons for an omelette filling; so many are needed that this is hardly worth while, though they have a delicate, distinctly mushroom flavour.

In a corner of the vegetable garden I found a clump of the honey fungus, *Armillaria mellea*, golden-brown and mushroom-shaped, the stems, nearly twenty in number, all growing up from the same base. As the older ones became tall and opened their caps more widely, they dropped their dead-white spores on to the younger ones below, like a coating of talcum powder.

In the gravel path, at the foot of a beech sapling stump, there had sprung up overnight a host of *Coprinus micaceus*, whose bright brown cone-shaped caps with vertically grooved edges varied in height from a half to one and a half inches. Both in their numbers and in the suddenness of their appearance there was something highly comic about them, standing in tiers, like spectators in a packed football stadium. But members of this genus have even shorter lives than most fungi. Within a day the edges of their caps were turning black, and two days later nothing remained but a slimy pool of disintegration.

At the top of the garden, beside the rhododendron hedge, there were a few representatives of larger species, *Boletus* and *Paxillus* and false chanterelles—invaders perhaps from the near-by heathlands. These are wooded with birch and Scots pine, both of which flourish in the acid sandy soil, and with the durmast oak. Gorse, especially the dwarf autumn-flowering kind, broom, bell heather, ling and cross-leaved heath, bracken and coarse tufted grass make up the lower levels of vegetation. Here *Boletus* and the larger agarics are at home.

Most conspicuous was the fly agaric, best-known toadstool in the world, to judge by the frequency of its suburban appearance in effigy alongside the bearded dwarf gardener. But such crude imitations completely miss the subtle form and colouring of these red-and-white spotted beauties as they come up freshly through the sandy soil with traces of their passage still dusting their caps. In appearance tempting enough to eat, they are nevertheless very poisonous, though not deadly in small quantities, for the Vikings are said to have chewed them to induce their berserk fits.

But we ate *Boletus*, of which there were several well-defined species. Large and mushroom-shaped, they have instead of plate-like gills a mass of minute tubes whose closely crowded openings give the underside of the cap a spongy appearance. First choice was the cep or stone fungus, the German *Steinpilz*, usually about six

Page 123 (above) Chamaemelum nobile; (right) Part of the garden at Lower Treneague

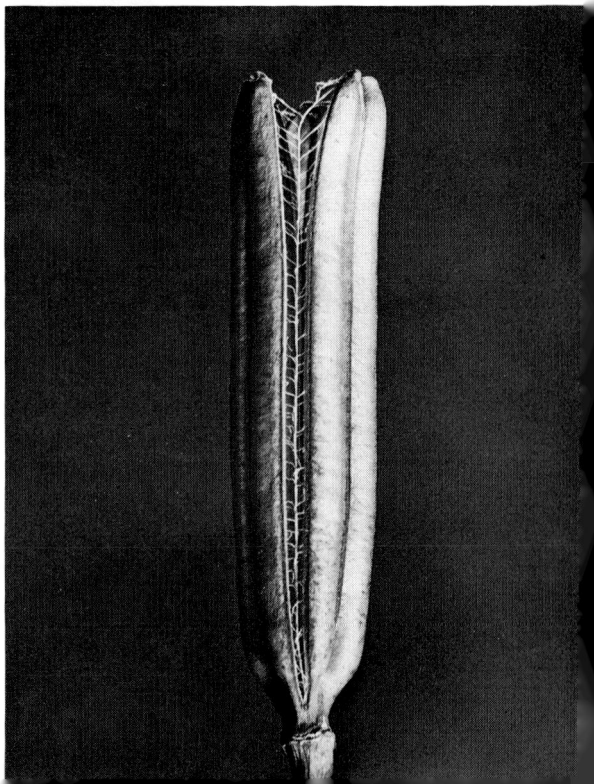

inches across, with a shiny brown top and distinctive bulbous stem. Our finest specimen, with a cap nearly a foot in diameter, its height being somewhat less, was growing in splendid isolation near a group of pines, far too much a king among *Boleti* for us to consider picking it for soup. 'Bun soup' it came to be called, for *Boletus* is like a well-baked bun in appearance. We found the larger specimens, mature but firm, to be best for cooking; the small and younger ones were easier to peel and the inedible tubes came away without difficulty from the flesh of the cap, but they were almost tasteless. The cep, *Boletus edulis*, at its best is delicious, with a strong mushroom flavour: it forms, in fact, the basis of many tinned and packet 'mushroom' soups.

Rather more abundant in our neighbourhood, among the birches, was *B scaber*, slightly smaller than the cep, with a longer thinner stem covered with greyish scales. The cap is dull brown and the tubes are whitish, somewhat unappetising in appearance; but this is a perfectly wholesome fungus. Occasionally we found one of an entirely whitish colour—an unbaked bun perhaps. From among the pines another species, whose yellow tubes and flesh turned to a poisonous-looking blue when bruised or cut, I decided must be *B badius*, with its bay-brown cap. In spite of its ominous appearance it too is perfectly wholesome.

Liable to be confused at first glance with *Boletus* was *Paxillus involutus*, especially as it was growing half-hidden in the heathery verges of the paths. But, though similar in size and colour, it has, instead of the yellow sponge underneath, deeply decurrent gills—that formation so strongly reminiscent of fan-vaulting—and the caps of the older ones become concave.

There were also other kinds of *Amanita*, less spectacular than the fly agaric, pushing up through the sand. A penny plain version was the poisonous *A pantherina*, whose whitish spots were on a dull brown instead of a scarlet background. Hardly distinguishable from it was *A rubescens*, the blusher, whose characteristic feature is that its flesh turns pink when cut. At the beginning of September, before the fungus flood had really begun, there were already quantities of blushers, but by October they had mostly disappeared.

The only true rival in brightness to the fly agaric was *Russula*, and beneath the pines the species most generously represented was the poisonous *R emetica*, with chalk-white gills and stem and bright carmine cap, fading to pink in old age. Other conspicuous, though smaller, denizens of the wooded heath included the yellow sulphur-tuft, *Hypholoma fasciculare*, growing in enormous crowded groups beside old oak stumps, and the bright orange *Calocera viscosa*, based on a rotting pine log and branched and erect like a small rubbery seaweed.

Near the heath runs the Basingstoke Canal, whose towpath is bordered with oak and alder-buckthorn, gorse, broom and brambles. *Boletus* and the fly agaric appeared among the waterside grasses, and one of the oaks was host to a fine, pale fawn *Pleurotus corticatus* protruding shelf-like from the trunk. By the middle of the month, at the foot of the same tree, one or two specimens of *Laccaria laccata* var *amethystina* were appearing, their caps, stems and gills all of the same pale mauve colour.

A path leading on to the heath joins the towpath at an open space covered with short grass—the favoured habitat of several more kinds of *Russula*. In addition to *R emetica* we found *R atropurpurea*, whose deep red-purple cap looked like a chestnut conker when it first emerged from the ground. *R drimeia* was similar in colouring, but its gills were pale yellow and its stem was tinged with purple instead of being pure white; *R azurea* had a bluish-green cap.

In contrast to neat symmetrical *Russula* were the woolly milk caps. About eight inches across, their pink caps were covered with a sort of straggling white felt, and the drops of white liquid from which they are named oozed from cuts and splits in the gills. In the same clearing we found common puffballs, mostly elderly specimens, two inches in diameter and of a dirty yellowish-brown, spotted with white where their juvenile spines had rubbed off. Finally, a group of elf-cups lay like pieces of thin orange peel on the turf.

Between the canal and the house is a wide no-man's-land, marshy, covered with cotton grass and heather, and pitted with brown peaty pools. It rises to an eminence in the shape of an ancient British hill-top camp—in fact an old rubbish dump overgrown with grass and nettles and with dandelions still blooming magnificently well into October. This heap of fertile earth had its own special fungus population: innumerable flourishing colonies of honey agaric, finer than those in the garden, and almost as many clumps of *Hypholoma velutinum*, whose brown caps have a spider-web fringe.

Eye-catching were the splendid lawyers' wigs, often more than a foot high, whose tall thin caps, greyish-white in colour, descend in concentric scaly circles to curl up at the lower edge. Larger relations of *Coprinus micaceus* in the garden path, they too disintegrated quickly. All the specimens we saw were already blackening and, though still handsome, were unfortunately too far gone on the road to liquescence to be fit for food. But there were plenty of the common ink cap, *C atramentarius*, in crowded colonies. It could be found in most stages of maturity, from the small firm cones to patches of bare stems with the last shreds of black decomposition dangling from them, looking like the aftermath of a forest fire in miniature.

Common ink caps are smaller than their shaggy relative, smooth-surfaced and pale greyish or brownish in colour, opening out from a cocoon shape to a narrow bell. I picked a pound or so of perfect specimens in a very few moments and, fried gently after peeling, they certainly gave us the illusion of a generous helping of the best, most delicate mushrooms. They should not be eaten after they have begun to turn black, and in some instances they have been known to cause mild poisoning and reddening of the face when taken with wine; but that was an experiment I did not make.

THE LUPIN KING   Ethel, Lady Thomson

Many years ago, when we lived on the outskirts of York, word went round the neighbourhood that we were on the look-out for a gardener. An elderly man who lodged near by in one of the monotonous new streets called one evening to say that he would come and help us out. I was immensely struck both by his appearance and by his manner. He was of the type of Albert Schweitzer, with an untidy moustache and spare figure, his speech and bearing full of authority and independence. He had a gentle, though slightly rasping, voice and a kind of hesitancy or catching of the breath in the middle of long sentences. Desperately serious in tone, he gave the impression that he would brook neither nonsense nor flippancy.

He told us that he rented an allotment 'up the road' at Bustardthorpe, half way between us and Bishopthorpe, and was carrying out horticultural experiments there: breeding lupins, in fact. As he spoke of his beloved studies and endeavours his blue eyes lit up with the gleam of enthusiasm, and from speaking of the wonders of nature in growth, beauty of form and colouring he would go on to talk of the scientific discoveries of Mendel in the laws relating to the breeding of species, human, animal and floral. One could see that the man had a touch of genius. This happy chance of a business relationship gave me the opportunity of becoming, in a short time, closely acquainted with George Russell.

Almost our first point of contact, beyond discussing the sowing of vegetables, was the information that he lived next door to a widow with an only son who was far from strong. The doctors recommended that he should live as much as possible in the open air—advice which the mother could not adopt unless she left the child outside on the pavement all day. George Russell solved the problem, much to the boy's delight, by putting him on a piece of sacking in the wheelbarrow with spade, fork, rake, hoe and any other tools he might require, and pushing the lad every morning up to his allotment, ten minutes' walk away, to play around while he worked. He told me that he dosed the child daily with lumps of sugar soaked with eucalyptus, two in the morning and two at night, which steadily improved his condition. As the years passed, 't'little lad', as George Russell called him, began to take note of what the old man was doing, and gradually learned about the growth and culture of lupins.

Meanwhile the allotment became a magnet drawing the attention of horticulturists from all over England and of many visitors from the continent and from America. Often on summer evenings we would stroll up to Bustardthorpe to be shown the progress George Russell was making and the many lovely colours he was producing from the original blues and whites. He would tell us proudly of the handsome offers he was constantly receiving from horticulturists who sought to buy his secrets; but he would not sell and the would-be purchasers went away disappointed. At last, as he grew into advanced old age, he thought he should retire and sold his entire stock to a Midland firm. They provided him with a cottage over-looking their gardens and made 't'little lad', who by this time had grown into a fine young man, custodian in chief of the valuable collection.

Why, I had sometimes wondered, had George Russell taken up such an original hobby at the late age of sixty. One day, without my asking any questions, he told me. He had suffered a great sorrow and a deep hurt to his pride and his feelings. I heard all the details and could only agree that they were very painful. To conquer all the disillusionment and heal the wounds under which his sensitive nature smarted, he took the courageous course of beginning life over again and throwing himself heart and soul into the culture and propagation of lupins. Happiness had come to him during his latter years, bringing success and public recognition. In the New Year's Honours of January 1951 he was awarded the MBE in acknowledge-ment of his services to horticulture. The following October he died at the ripe age of ninety-four.

SPRING-CABBAGE PLANTING

> The dibble, like a sharp-beaked bird,
> Pecked at the rough and stony ground.
> Planting in autumn for spring, I heard
> The voice of winter in the sound,
> Insistent as grief,
> Of the falling leaf.
>
> Like lines of faith in a book of prayer,
> At the end of the chill and doubtful day
> The plants in ordered rows stood there,
> Shining against lack-lustre clay
> Whose vellum page
> Was dull with age.

The sky cleared for a coming frost;
A robin clinked his last sad stave.
The sun in western mist was lost.
The field became a shadowy grave
From which the last
Mourner has passed.

G. J. Blendell

TAIL CORN

Garden boy, ruefully surveying weedy border: 'There ain't nobody
what wouldn't think that 'ere bed 'adn't bin wed last week.'

WINTER

WAX FLOWERS

At first you might think they were real. The
                artist gathered
All that he could from nature, day by day
Watching her changing moods—now fine, now
                fathered
By sudden storms into wild disarray:
The fallen petal, the tousled bloom he noted,
Prised the most intimate secrets of the bud,
Marked where the bee made entry, honey-coated,
And came to his mute wax eager as a god.

It seemed a unique achievement. But lay a finger
On that cool lily, touch the lizard skin
Spotted with gold: there is no answering languor,
Nothing to lure the moth's sleek presence in,
And all the hurrying seasons' joyful press
Finds but an empty husk of perfectness.

Jean Kenward

THE TREE THROUGH THE WINDOW
Norman Dawson

I cannot remember the time when trees, seen through the window,
did not mean more to me than the house I lived in. My first days
were spent in a Lancashire cotton town where mill-chimneys were
more frequent than trees. The windows of our house looked over a
flagged pavement that rang with the clatter of clogs four times a day
when the weaving sheds opened their gates. But across the cobbled
street was a churchyard, and in the churchyard a tree. By country
standards it was not much of a tree; it was stunted and black with
soot. But all my memories of those years are in terms of the annual
cycle of that tree. When it was leafless and bare, that meant potato-
cakes or muffins for tea, a high-banked fire, the gas lit early, and
hours playing with paints on the hearthrug. When it showed its

first pale green buds—it was a pink hawthorn—that was a sign for the gnawing fever that sent me out, first by electric tram and then for many miles on foot, to the Pennine extremities of the cotton-belt, to search in the scraggy and soiled cloughs and denes for the natural joys that instinct but not experience told me should have been my birthright. There were even pure streams and trout to tickle, if you got far enough into the hills above the bleachworks and dyeworks. You could find bluebells, if you knew where to look and kept your secret well.

When the tree began to show colour in its buds, that was the time for the town-dwellers, the troglodytes, to come out into the air. There would soon be men in their shirt-sleeves playing bowls on the nearby green. The little girls appeared with whips and tops, and the teenagers (unknown word then) strolled with their tennis rackets down to the recreation ground, looking at each other with slanting eyes. By the time the faded pink flowers were falling, it was warm enough for the air, always pulsing with the beat of a myriad looms, to carry with each throb the musky, feminine scent of damp cotton. Memory is less sure about the tree in the autumn months. But when I recall my mother telling me quietly, on 4 August 1914, that war had been declared, I remember the tree in full and dingy leaf, dripping under a drab and pitiless rain that might have been intended to epitomise the next five years.

Oxford brought my first acquaintance with real trees, as, indeed, with blue skies as well. My clearest memory of those years is neither of the men I met nor of the comely, grey-stone college piles, but of what seemed to me then to be rampant greenery, and above all of a single mock-acacia leaning out from a corner of the college quadrangle. I saw my first nuthatch clinging to its bark. I did not realise until long after that I probably owed that tree to the opinionated Cobbett. It is more than twenty years since I saw it, but I saw only a few days ago in the press a reproduction of a pen-and-wash drawing of that quadrangle. The tree is still there, but sadly mutilated. The great curving branch that used almost to sweep the turf sacred to the Senior Common Room is now but a cut stump.

After Oxford I had many temporary homes, and those of which

my recollection is faintest are those where there was no tree. The first home I was free to choose for myself was sought out doggedly and with a fierce conviction. It was in the midst of ancient woodland; but it had, peculiar to itself, two trees. One was a yew, natural-grown and innocent of the shears, that made a green gloom of our kitchen. It was worth it. I remember a spring when that yew-tree held a wren's nest in a cleft in its twisted trunk, a spotted flycatcher's at the end of a horizontal branch, a blackbird's in a fork, two untidy sparrow-piles halfway up, a thrush's, a goldfinch's and, almost at the utmost tip, a goldcrest's. We heard the gold-crests long before we saw them; once they were found they were easy to watch from the simplest of hides—a bedroom window.

The second tree was a colossal beech. It remains in memory a Laocoon tangle of great roots utterly absorbing the eye through a little scullery window. When one looks at a beech out-of-doors, inevitably the eye is drawn up the smooth trunk until it loses itself in the green dome above. But from inside that window the one focal point was framed, where the great creature gripped the earth and strangled it. One stared through the window, across the sink, hypnotised by the creeping terror of vegetable growth.

My next home, the sequel to a battle between instinct and necessity, was in a garden suburb that had over-run an ancient orchard. The tree was a greengage. It bore no fruit, nor did I in that environment.

And now, for thirteen seasons, I have watched the spring come and touch with long, late plumes the dearest tree of all. It is an ash. It must be all of a hundred and thirty years old. Its topmost boughs are stark and dead, and their finer twigs have long gone as building material for the nearby rookery. I am looking at it now, as I lie in bed nursing a minor illness. It is framed in the casement, and in its turn it frames with its drunken limbs a range of snow-tipped fells against a winter sky. I know, as I look at it, that wherever I go that outline will stay etched on my memory. When we were young, we used to put flowers or ferns in a photographic printing frame together with a sensitised sheet, expose them to the sun and get a brilliant image in white that we fixed with hypo. Well, the hypo of my memory has done that for the ash, but in black, not white, and against a brilliant western sky. I can still picture the line of a high-reaching branch that foundered in an autumn gale, it must be three years ago. That was hard luck for the rooks, for they have shared my affection for the ash, and that branch—the topmost tip of it—had been for years the chairman's perch for the autumn convocations. The chairman has had to move down a peg now, but the convocations still go on, broken at intervals by unseemly brawls. And I know, too, that they will go on, in my memory, whether once again I have to move on, or whether the power that now rules all our destinies—the county council—decrees the compulsory felling of the ash. For an upstart arterial road now runs below, and the tree's tired limbs shake with the vibration of heavy transport, thundering north.

NEGLECTED TREES   J. D. U. Ward

It has been said that the English love trees but dislike forests. I wonder. Tree-felling and branch-lopping anywhere, at any time, are liable to produce howls of protest which might suggest affection; yet many trees are shamefully treated without compunction. Picnic fires are lit against them, nails and staples driven into them and barbed wire wrapped round them. But perhaps most significant of all is the lack of positive care bestowed on them and of discrimination—readiness to exploit opportunities—in planting them.

Much of the beauty of ornamental trees depends on their shape, but really well-grown specimens, whose form and condition reveal that some knowledgeable person has tended them, are not nearly as common as one would expect in a nation of tree-lovers. The stock saying is, 'I like trees to look natural.' Examination of that word 'natural' might lead to many awkward questions: here it must suffice to say that trees which 'naturally' grow in dense competition are not being so treated when they are well spaced for development or grouped specially to please the eye. As a general rule it is desirable to remove some of the lower branches and to shorten others from an early age—work often begun too late—both to encourage the leader to grow despite the absence of 'natural' competition and to give the tree a clean bole. The species of tree, the site, the proximity and character of the nearest trees and other circumstances vary so widely that little general advice can be offered; but obviously a small wound heals more quickly than a large one, and drastic amputations are undesirable, though sometimes necessary after prolonged neglect.

How many corners of land carrying trees or lying waste and odd half-acres at the bottom of country gardens are planted as they might be? The ubiquitous purple-leaved plum and the Kanzan cherry reveal a liking for fast-growing trees that make a show, but they do not suggest discrimination or a cultivated taste. It is easy, however, to scold or find fault: constructive suggestions may be more useful. The success of two species, the Lombardy poplar introduced barely two hundred years ago and more recently acquired Irish yew, suggests that we might pay more attention to erect-branched forms. The fastigiate oak, for example, is pleasing, yet might almost be called a rarity. The Dawyck beech is not quite so scarce, and semi-fastigiate forms of the London plane have been used in street planting, but erect-growing varieties of birch, hornbeams, false-acacia and tulip tree are rare in most of Britain.

Also neglected are the cut-leaved varieties of some common trees, notably the extremely beautiful beech. I cannot recall having seen a single specimen of what is usually called the fern-leaved oak within fifty miles of where I write. The cut-leaved silver birch is also pretty but uncommon. Incidentally few trees provide more apt illustrations of neglect and ignorance than the birches. They seem to be everywhere, and nearly everywhere they are ill-shaped and ill-grown. For its bark the silver birch, *Betula verrucosa* is to be preferred to the white *B pubescens*, and anyone free of the ridiculous prejudice against 'alien' trees may choose *B papyrifera*, whose silvery-white bark the North American Indians used for their canoes.

In a damp place or to overhang a stream, the cut-leaved alder is an excellent tree; its foliage might almost be plumage, so feathery does it seem. It is not now very common, for it has been planted less freely in the last fifty years than in a period 1770–1840. The influence of fashion on tree-planting is often forgotten. Another quite different but beautiful water-loving tree, the so-called swamp cypress (it is not a true cypress) had a spell of popularity in the eighteenth and early nineteenth centuries but has since been relatively ignored; its leaves retain a fresher green in August than those of any other tree I know and turn to a good reddish-rust before they fall. This, by the way, is one of the few trees which will flourish with its roots in water all the year round. Yet another tree for wet spots is the ring-leaved weeping willow var *annularis*. For W. J. Bean it had 'little beauty', but that is a matter of taste. At Kew, looking at a good specimen with completely ringleted leaves, I marvelled that anything so attractive and easily propagated should be so uncommon.

Of curious foliage is the eagle's claw maple, a variety of the Norway maple var *laciniatum* which might with advantage replace many an ordinary sycamore or scrubby birch. The small Japanese maples and some purple-leaved varieties are planted in hundreds of gardens, but one sees certain of the larger and no less beautiful species much less often. Even the lovely and fast-growing silver maple, though planted in public parks, is much less appreciated than it should be. The red maple var *sanguineum* and the *reitenbachii* variety of Norway maple are both trees which deserve more recognition.

Some members of the genus *Sorbus* are well known: the mountain ash or rowan must be one of the most popular of all decorative trees, and the whitebeam, which locally has the apt name of white-and-fair, may be seen far from the chalk which it specially loves; indeed it competes with the rowan for the verges of suburban roads. But the two species which provide the finest autumn colour and also some of the largest trees, the service tree and the wild service tree, are rare over most of England, though in parts of Kent and Sussex the latter, whose leaves are more like maple than ash or rowan, is locally fairly common. Not even the briefest reference to autumn colour can be closed without mention of the red gum tree *Liquidambar styraciflua*. It grows rather slowly but is beautiful while small; anyone who wants to know what his great-grandchildren may enjoy can see the largest specimens in England at Syon House, across the river from Kew. Three trees which make a good display in both spring and autumn are our native wild cherry or gean, the American rum cherry and the Japanese cherry, *P sargentii*; they are also useful timber-producers.

Almost every tree I have mentioned should achieve a height of fifty feet or more and may be planted in company with economic trees where contrast, ornament or variety is needed, as at the corner of a wood, the meeting of rides or any place where people habitually go to enjoy a view.

THE DEVIL AMONG THE LETTUCES   Michael Bird

There are not many references in English literature to lettuces. Apart from their soporific effect on the Flopsy Bunnies, readers would be hard put to it to find mention in their qualities. Certainly few would ascribe a satanic nature to them. Yet one of our earliest books describes the devil as dwelling in a lettuce.

In her biography of Alfred the Great, Eleanor Duckett tells how the king, in order to fortify the faith of his sorely-tried subjects, caused Bishop Werferth to translate the dialogues of St Gregory into the native Anglo-Saxon tongue. First among the stories which the saint relates to his doubting deacon Peter is that of a nun who ate a lettuce without first blessing it. She was seized with a violent stomach-ache which was diagnosed as a case of demonic possession. The other sisters straightway sent for a certain Holy Equitus, who came at great speed. No sooner had he arrived than the devil called out from the poor nun's mouth: 'What have I done? I was merely sitting in the lettuce and she came and ate me.' The Holy Equitus thereupon bade the devil in the name of God to depart and he did so, never to return.

On reading this simple tale my thoughts went back to the time during the war when I lay in a military hospital next to a captain. He held a commission in the Iraq levies, who were of mixed races and religions. 'Our Christians, mostly Assyrians, give little trouble and will eat anything,' he said. 'The Moslems will not touch pork, of course. Then there are the Yezidis; they will not eat lettuce.'

They are devil worshippers dwelling near Mosul. The founders of their religion decided that it was better to come to terms with the powers of evil than actively to seek the power of good; and for this faith they are prepared to face persecution and martyrdom at the hands of true believers.

'But why eschew lettuce?' I asked.

'It is like this,' my friend replied. 'They believe that Satan was originally one of the angels, but that he fell from grace. He was chased from Heaven by the Archangel Gabriel with a sharp spear and, on reaching Earth, took refuge in the heart of a lettuce. Gabriel's spear easily pierced the frail leaves, and the wounded devil had to flee. He then found safety in a large onion whose slippery scales were proof against the darts of the Archangel.' Thus the father of lies survived to carry on his mischief, and his worshippers came to despise the lettuce and hold the onion in the highest regard.

'Those Yezidis are a strange lot' went on the captain. 'Although they worship the devil they are most trustworthy and honest. They think it best never to mention the name of the evil one; and instead of representing him in a grotesque form they humour him by depicting him as a peacock.'

THE LUCK OF THE YEAR   Geoffrey Grigson

Last spring I saw for the first time a wood floored with wild lilies of the valley. How thoroughly it was one of those sights by which existence is renewed! They were not the first of which I had ever had experience. I have seen them in stranger conditions, on pavements of mountain limestone in the west of Yorkshire, the leaves clattering together in the wind—delightful, yet a little bizarrely unnatural, offering satisfaction of a different kind in a region of uncommon plants growing uncommonly out of cracks of limestone. Entering a wood, not otherwise unlike any other wood, and finding instead of nettles or white garlic these slender and pure lilies by the acre was a renewal for a short while not only of existence, but of the familiar plant itself, native and more delicate than lilies-of-the

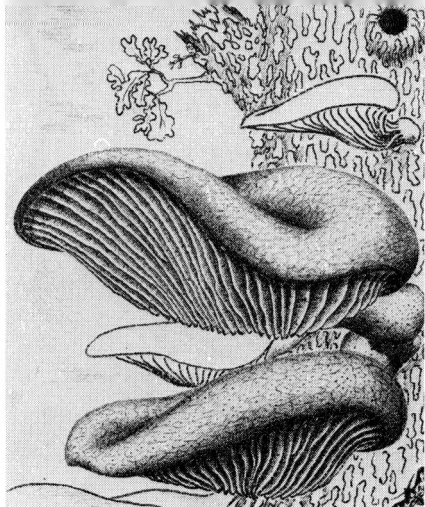

Page 142 (above right) Paxillus involutus; (above left) Pleurotus corticatus; (below) Coprinus micaceus

valley in a garden bed. It was the difference between a real nymph and a marble nymph, if not between a tiger burning in the jungle which is its proper habitat and a tiger at Regent's Park.

Quite a number of plants can be renewed in this way from familiarity in the garden; and I was lucky with them last spring. At the end of May I stopped by another wood which I knew vaguely to be famous among botanists. A few yards in, under the oak trees, were clumps of Solomon's Seal. Pleasantly and formally as this more odd plant undoes and spreads its leaves in a garden corner,

Wild Lily-of-the-Valley

the site is too often dry and shabby, lending its dryness and shabbiness all too soon to the whole plant. Here in the wood each bent-over stem was wet and vivid. The young seals—the flowers, green and white—were each beaded with raindrops. Sometimes a plant curved up between two roots of a tree. My first impression was of grace coupled with the regularity of the leaves and seals. However, the clumps were scattered, one here, one there, about twenty or thirty yards apart. The second impression was of groups of old women hunched together in the rain and resigned to a hard life, as they might be in a sentimental picture of toil by Millet and Legros.

I went to this wood again two days later, in sunshine, and stumbled on a brilliant patch of lungwort. It was not the lungwort of the New Forest with narrow leaves, which is a true native, but the naturalised *Pulmonaria officinalis*, which, in gardens and in full light, is apt again to look dry and shabby. I do not know how it came into the wood, whether by chance or design. But the blue of the flowers—some are red, some blue—was deeper and more

Solomon's Seal

healthy altogether. The green of the lung-spotted leaves had a freshness I have never observed. Solomon's Seal hunched itself beyond this wide patch of lungwort—an extraordinary contrast in kind and colour.

The luck of the year held. Some days later, on a damp evening, I drove out to a peculiar stream which rises below the chalk and turns muddy and slow through flattish beds of clay. I do not mind the clay and mud and sloth, since the deep banks of the stream are fossiliferous to a degree. Immense belemnites stick out, sharp as a needle, with shells of an oyster-like creature, and bits of coralline rock from the low hills, dating from the era when this was a shallow tropical sea with coral reefs. Best of all the fossils is a small one which looks like a primeval catkin or the minute cone of some kind of fir. A few inches long, it tapers to a point at one end and finishes at the other in what you would take for a stem. In fact it is (or it was) animal, not vegetable, the spine of a creature called *Cidaris florigemma*—a pretty, intriguing object, ridged from tip to tip with pimples of stone. The trouble is always to find one which is perfect. I have never done so yet. I have the tapering ends and I have the stem ends. Bank after bank, beach after beach I tried,

Lungwort, *pulmonaria officinalis*

getting filthy with yellow mud and blue clay. Then I thought of a point farther downstream at the entrance to a shallow valley. Here the brook was banked up artificially and cascaded from beneath the road in a waterfall with a high bank, much broken, on either side. Down there I drove.

I searched the banks and the beach; there was no *Cidaris florigemma*, or at least only a few odds and ends. But under the alder trees, among nettles and willow-herb and comfrey, I did notice a slender and unusual plant—several plants—looking as wild as could be. It was easily recognised when I had crossed the brook and two fences of barbed wire and waded through a bed of nettles and had it in my hands: nothing but *Aconitum napellus* or monkshood, commonplace of gardens, native in the south and south-west occasionally, but not in this Wiltshire countryside. Nothing but *Aconitum napellus*—that is entirely wrong. It was monkshood with a difference, more slender, more delicate than the coarse plants in my own garden; naturalised, if not wild, holding its own perfectly well in a natural community of vegetation.

When I got home I turned up monkshood in the county flora, sixty-three years old. There it was, recorded for the same parish, observed no doubt in the same place below the waterfall, though the entry was meanly hedged between brackets to indicate that it was only an escape—correct, no doubt, though I saw no house near it or the waterfall. But it is a good thing always to have one of the early nineteenth-century maps of the district you live in. I turned to the one-inch map of 1828, which gave the secret. There had been a mill just across the road, and in all likelihood the plant had escaped— how many years ago?—from the miller's garden. Next time I went there I found the dry mill leat going along the side of the valley.

Monkshood

One discovery leads to another, which is part of the perpetual novelty of the most familiar countryside. As well as finding the monkshood, I had picked a large bunch of comfrey, purple-flowered and white-flowered, which I thought might look well in a vase. It did nothing of the kind, promptly wilting before breakfast, as do many plants in the same family. Then our Bavarian maid noticed the wilted vaseful. 'Schwarzwurzel!' she said with what I thought unnecessary excitement. 'Schwarzwurzel! We eat that at home.' Black root or rough leaf, I could not fancy that it was very good to eat. But there I was wrong; it does not do to underestimate German folk cookery. Our Bavarian dipped the leaves into water, then into a pancake batter, and fried them quickly and crisply, a little disappointed that we should not be eating them in the proper way, which is with sauerkraut. One by one they came out of the frying pan, tapering and slender, half golden, half viridian, like fillets of some tropical fish. With sugar or without, they tasted well, a little juicy, not at all rough as you might expect, and decidedly fresh, which is the nearest description of a flavour individual yet not easy to define.

You should try these Schwarzwurzel pancakes, which Bavarian farmers eat by the plateful. Comfrey, after all, is one of the commonest plants by the waterside all over England, and one of the easiest to recognise. Every time I now see this coarse and commonplace herb, between spring and December, it will have for me a new personality.

POOR MEN'S FLOWERS
Alan Walbank with drawings by John Nash, RA

Among the tributes that we are paying nowadays to the Victorians one has been overlooked that should be paid in flowers. It is due not to the eminent in art or science but to the humbly anonymous artisan. When, just before Queen Victoria's accession, Cobbett observed that the taste for making pretty gardens had been declining in England for many years, he spoke as one who had started life as garden boy at Farnham Castle. Between the old formal gardens and elaborate landscape gardening the gentry might indeed seem to have lost touch, nor could their mid-century cult of hothouse exotics be called real garden interest. Those faithful recorders of the middle classes, Dickens, Thackeray and George Eliot, have little to say about their activities as gardeners. It seems unlikely that they were as passionately attached to their gardens as we are today, or that they thought half as much of flowers 'as individuals and dear friends' as of rolling their gravel walks.

It is the artisan who deserves most of the credit for keeping alive and transmitting interest in our favourite garden flowers, especially those of spring. With them he had a strong traditional connexion from the first, for the colony of Flemish weavers who held a florists' feast in Norwich in 1637 started a fashion that spread to other manufacturing towns and provoked a fruitful rivalry. Tulips, auriculas, polyanthuses, pinks, hyacinths, sweet williams and ranunculuses were the flowers that received early attention, and individually they exerted great local fascination.

In Lancashire the silk weavers of Middleton raised remarkable edged auriculas, grey, green and white. Manchester and Macclesfield workers devoted themselves particularly to gold-laced and silver-laced polyanthuses. The skill and invention of operatives at Paisley and Falkirk seem to have carried over from the manufacture of fancy fabrics to the cultivation of the choicest variegated pinks. 'No shaded, run-off, pin-eyed thing' would do for the weaver, says Crabbe, but 'the brilliant hues are all distinct and clean. No kindred tints, no blending streaks between.' Precise shape, colour and colour pattern were the qualities that appealed to the craftsman, and in these his chosen flowers offered endless experimentation. So with sweet williams, which had been recommended by a member of the Gardeners' Society in 1722 for cultivating in built-up areas on London clay, it was the auricula-eyed variety that was favoured. The double ranunculus was also highly regarded and, according to William Howitt, especially so among Derbyshire villagers in the early nineteenth century. He notes that some of the finest ranunculuses, polyanthuses and pinks bore the names of cottage florists who were scarcely ever out of their own

Choicest variegated pinks

districts. Such flowers as these were 'poor men's flowers', remarked Loudon, 'and a fine blow was rarely seen in the gardens of the nobility and gentry'.

To this artisan tradition the Victorian miner and weaver, cottager and small tradesman added new wealth. Two circumstances favoured the hobby when resources and leisure were so restricted. A worker housed in a cottage orné on one of the new great estates would no doubt be encouraged to add to its decorative appearance. In industrial areas the pursuit won approval because it took men

Geraniums in a cottage window

out of gin and beer shops and did something to uplift their minds. The growing of these small flowers did not demand much room among crowded tenements and in fact has been called 'the last solace of art for the slums'. So, although Victorian writers had little to remark about gardening activity among the middle classes, we find them recognising its place in humbler lives. A retired tradesman, for example, in a novel of the fifties by Anne Marsh, is endowed with a small cottage at the back of Hampstead Heath where he spends his time raising prize carnations, auriculas and ranunculuses. How much better it is, the author adds, to see thrift and industry getting pleasure out of small things than to have high wages, luxury and low morals! In Boz's sketch of London recreations two garden-owners are contrasted: the City man who never does anything to his garden with his own hands, but descants about the cost of maintaining it; and the old couple in Kilburn Road who fondly tend hyacinths in the parlour window and geraniums in the forecourt.

Geraniums and other pelargoniums, dahlias (newly introduced from abroad), and the show pansy (developed at home from the old heartsease) were some of the other flowers to which the working man devoted his labour of love. Geraniums were soon in every cottage window, more various than in the scarlet parterres of politer gardens, and pansy societies sprang up apace, chiefly among miners, to whose lasting fondness for small flowers D. H. Lawrence was witness. In *Sons and Lovers* he plants their gardens near Nottingham with auriculas, sweet williams, saxifrages and pinks; when the miner's wife buys pansies and crimson daisies to set, there is a special note of rapture.

The poets too reflected the poor man's taste and even took sides with him against 'the dreary botanical titles of exotic plants in the hothouse'. So Clough declared for daisies, violets, lilies and heartsease, regarding with disfavour the newer cult of the dahlia. Alexander Smith, who was brought up at Paisley and was, like his father, a pattern-designer, recalled a garden scene of white lilies and freaked pansies in the 'thousand-streeted smoke-smothered town,' and Matthew Arnold spoke affectionately of the musk carnation, the gold-dusted snapdragon and sweet williams with their 'homely cottage smell'. This sympathy and feeling are perhaps nowhere better revealed than in that popular mid-Victorian ballad, 'I'm a Broken-hearted Gardener,' as he sings of his choice:

> *She's my snowdrop, my ranunculus,*
> *My hyacinth, my gillyflower, my polyanthus,*
> *My heartsease, my pink, my water-lily,*
> *My buttercup, my daisy, my daffy-down-dilly.*

Many of our garden flowers owe their present beauty and variety to the fond enthusiasms of working men who also experimented endlessly with them. Browning's Pippa alone seems to have regretted the passing of the simple heartsease into something more rare.

GROWING A WALNUT TREE   E. M. Seal

Out of a precious war-time pound of walnuts I saved two to plant in November. One grew, the shoot appearing in the following spring, and when we moved to another house with a large garden I took the young tree. It had grown only about 18in in two years but had surpassed all expectations in downward growth. After exposing 2ft of tap-root without any sight of the end I decided I could go no farther, and as there were numerous hair roots I cut it and filled in the large hole.

I had been warned by a trusted nurseryman that a tree grown from seed would not produce walnuts till it was fifteen years old, unless it were grafted. However, I like walnut trees for many other things. The young curled-over bronze leaves are delightful; the tree, unless mutilated, has a robust spread like an oak's; and when one brushes against the large, handsome, pinnate leaves they give out a pleasant perfume. These are benefits enough while you are waiting for fruit. Besides, there is the pleasure of watching the tree grow.

When it was nine years old and the leaves had fallen there was one nut. This was a mystery, for next year, before the leaves were fully expanded, I noticed many female buds but no male catkin, and I remembered enough school botany to know that both are borne on the same tree. There is, however, a mature tree not far away. From this I collected some fallen catkins, and when the stigmas on my young tree were large enough I pollinated them with an old shaving brush. While I did so I pondered on the remarkable chance which had led to the production of the previous year's nut, as the pollen presumably had to come 150yds from the old tree. That season the tree produced fifteen nuts. The following year male catkins appeared before the leaf-buds broke, and I felt my role of *deus ex machina* was now finished, especially when the crop numbered eighty-five.

We are fortunate in the quality of the fruit, the nuts being large and meaty. They could so easily have been meagre and would then have been only right for pickling, for which the large ones are unsuitable. It is a chance one has to take when growing from seed, and that is why the nurserygrown trees are always grafted; but the gamble makes the venture all the more exciting.

THE GHOST AND THE WALNUT TREE Eric Gatfield
(recounted to his neighbour Judith Butler of Clacton-on-Sea)

Forty years ago, when I was working with my father, we had to go and renovate an old house at Great Holland which had belonged to a very old lady, rich and a little eccentric. She was fond of children and cats, and the local children knew that any stray found and taken to her would earn them half a crown. In the end they used to get hold of her own cats and take them back to her for the money.

When she first went there, she had planted a walnut tree seven feet from the wall of the house. By the time she died at the age of ninety-three that tree was enormous, and it branches overlapped the roof; so our first job for the new owner was to cut it down. Gallons of water came out of the tree when we began to lop the branches. An old labourer came up to us and said: 'If you cut that tree down, the old lady'll come back and haunt the place. She near worshipped that tree—wouldn't let anyone touch it.' 'Don't be ridiculous,' my father said, and got on with the job.

Seven of us were working on the alterations, and shortly afterwards we began to hear footsteps on the stairs and a woman's voice talking to children or cats—perfectly clear, yet there was nobody to be seen. We used to go up and down stairs and all round the house, inside and out, and there was never anything to account for the sounds. One day we were all having tea in the dining-room. It was winter, so we had lit a fire and got a couple of trestles and a plank for a table. As we were sitting eating our tea, there came a great bang-bang on the window, like somebody knocking. We went out and searched all round, but there was no sign of anyone. The house stood by itself on the common, so there was no place where anyone could have been hiding.

One of the men, an elderly bricklayer, cried like a child. He had been frightened of ghosts as a little boy, and this brought back all the memories, which completely upset him. I told him that it was only someone playing a game; but he said he was going to give up his job. He did too; off he went, and he didn't come back. Next the electrician took to knocking off work every afternoon about half past three, as soon as it began to grow dark. Finally only my father and I would do a full day there; we worked by candle-light until six o'clock in spite of the mysterious footsteps and the woman's voice. These were so clear and ordinary that, when I was painting the bedrooms, I thought several times that someone was coming up to have a word with us. I would go and open the door; then the voice would stop, and there would be no one there.

Word got round that the place was haunted, and the owner could not sell it. At last he managed to let it to two ladies, a music teacher and her daughter, who ran it as a guest-house. They stayed there for twelve months and then left, because they couldn't stand it. At all hours of the night, they said, the old lady would be heard coming up the stairs, saying: 'Hello darling, what have you brought me? Have you brought me a lovely pussy then?'

All this time the walnut tree lay outside. Two men had dug a great pit and got the roots up, and it was lying across the hole. The owner got in touch with a firm of timber merchants, and one of them came down and offered thirty pounds for it. He was not only a member of the family firm but also a minister, so we told him what had been going on. 'Once the tree is carted away,' he said, 'and the roots burned, and the hole filled in and levelled, so that nothing of the tree is left, you'll probably find that the haunting will gradually cease.'

That is just what happened. A little later, when the tree had been removed, my father and I had to go and paint the outside of the house, and there was nothing odd about the place at all.

MOLE-TRAP

When we arrived the trap was empty.
An hour later, after we had talked
And admired the view, we walked
On the lawn and found him lying limply,
A fat prelatical mole
With pudgy pink hands.
While we were chatting politely, his sands
Had run out. His velvet was cool
Already to touch. He was a nuisance,
Spoiling the lawn with his heaps of earth,
Unlicensed upheavals like the birth
Of garden volcanoes. Sentence
Of death had to be passed, no doubt,
And had been carried out.
It was sentimental to regret
That clerical-looking rogue. And yet . . .

Ruth Bidgood

HOME-GROWN ROSES   **Hamish Batten**

Part of the enjoyment in gardening is the pleasure of being able to give away treasured plants and to receive from one's friends in return. Most of us are continually propagating our favourites, either from home-saved seed or by division, layering and cuttings of both stem and root. Perhaps too few attempt the supposedly more ambitious methods of grafting and budding, often dismissed as too difficult or as jobs for experts. Yet with roses neither is true.

You can search the hedgerows for suitable specimens of the dog-rose, but it is probably more convenient to buy from a specialist nurseryman, as his seedling stocks will be more uniform in size and vigour. They arrive in bundles looking like bunches of hedge trimmings. Each seedling stock will have three or four slender green stems arising from a bare neck up to 2in long and bearing a spray of wiry brown roots. The understocks may be heeled in the open ground temporarily, but by early March they should be planted out 1ft apart with 2ft 6in or so between the rows. The ground selected should be in good heart but not recently manured, as rank growth before budding is not desirable. Plant obliquely at 70° and leave the root-free neck initially above soil level, then earth it up by ridging to keep the bark supple. In this way the neck will be readily accessible when the bud is inserted in July. In the interval the beds need no attention beyond occasional hoeing; if space is pressing, a catch crop of lettuce or early cabbage may be taken between the rows before the top growth becomes too dense.

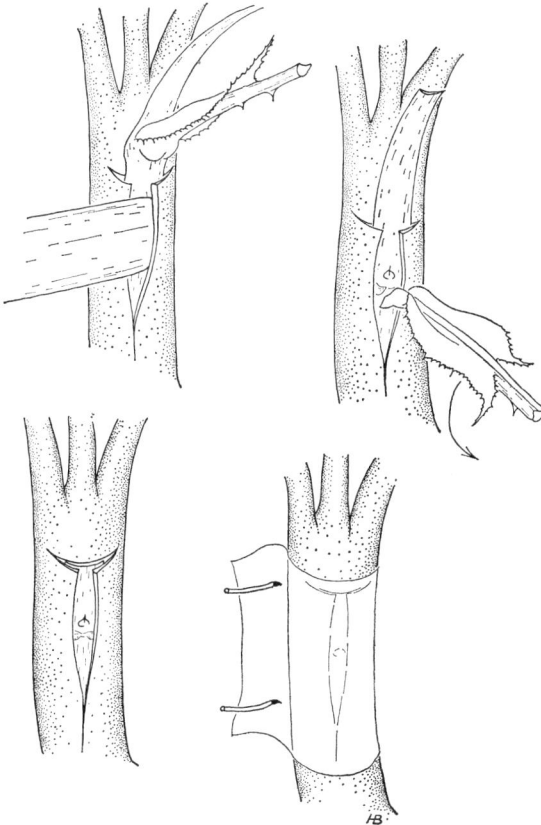

Budding roses

By early July the stocks will be ready for budding. For this the essentials are a really sharp budding knife or a scalpel, a stick of buds from the selected HT or floribunda rose, and a dash of courage to get you started. Select the stick from a stem cut 10in below a fading bloom. The buds in the axils of the upper two or three leaves will be either too thin or already breaking into shoots, depending on the habit of the variety; but those in the lower leaf axils should be at a suitable stage, preferably no more than a millimetre in height. By cutting off the leaves half an inch from the main stem transpiration will be reduced, so that the budding material may be transported suitably wrapped in polythene, or stored in water for two days if need be.

In outline, taking the bud consists of removing a thin shield of bark and wood by means of a shallow horizontal slicing cut, starting half an inch below the petiole or leaf stalk and ending the same distance above it, with a stripping movement. The stump of the petiole offers a convenient handle when removing the sliver of pale cream woody tissue on the inner surface of the bud shield. This operation is more safely carried out in two stages: first by pulling gently downwards the wood above the bud then, after reversing the shield in the hand, by detaching the segment of wood below the bud. With care and practice the wood may be removed successfully without damage to the critical embryo; this lies immediately behind the external bud and appears as a pin head, pale green and flattened, from which the new shoot will grow. Every bud must be inspected and, if the embryo is loosened or torn out, the shield must be discarded and new attempts made. A little practice on flower stems removed when dead-heading will soon perfect this technique.

When you feel competent to start, draw back the earth from a line of stocks and clean the neck of each with a damp rag. Being much slower than the skilled professional, I prefer to work in early morning or evening when evaporation from the cut surfaces of bud and stock is less rapid. An old raincoat thrown over the adjacent line of stocks will save you from painful embarrassment when bending down.

With the knife make a transverse cut in the bark across the neck of the stock about one-third of an inch below the origin of the stems, and from its centre a vertical cut downwards for an inch. Reverse the knife and trace its flat handle up the vertical cut ending with a twist movement, to lift slightly the cut edges of the bark. Having prepared a fresh bud shield, replace the knife handle just under the bark to ease its entry. Then, holding the petiole in the other hand, insert the shield behind the bark to the full depth of the vertical cut. If on inspection the bud fits neatly against the wood of the stock and is evenly covered by the bark, the petiole may be detached by bending it downwards and twisting gently; to prevent accidental displacement of the bud, hold together the upper edges of the cut bark with the free hand. Now trim off the protruding length of bud shield by retracing the knife over the horizontal cut.

The final stage of securing the inserted bud may be completed with one of the new plastic budding ties imported from Germany. Each consists of a short length of thin plastic film which is simply wrapped over the inserted bud and secured at the back of the stock with a wire staple. The light even tension of the stretched tape keeps the bud in place, reduces water loss from, and infection of, the cut surfaces and hastens the union of the cambial tissues. Further protection may be gained by replacing the earth to cover the ties for a few weeks. A 15in length of wide moistened raffia may be bound round the neck in place of the plastic tie, leaving a gap of an eighth of an inch over the bud itself. When raffia is to be used, do not remove the petiole, and smear the exposed bud with vaseline before earthing up.

In field practice the plastic ties are left on and eventually perish after a few months, but I prefer to remove them in September to examine the inserted bud. If the shield is still bright green (or at least the same colour as the parent stem) and the cut edges of bark show a rippled line of new callus, the bud has 'taken' and may be left to harden off.

The bud will usually stay dormant until the following spring, but a minority may even break into growth within a few weeks of insertion and produce in the same year short shoots ending in flowers. These 'springers' need careful marking with canes, to which the supple new growth must be tied; and in the following spring they must be cut hard back to within half an inch of their origin to induce dormant basal buds to break. If, on the other hand, the inserted bud has become a shrivelled brown shield, obviously dying, there is still time in September to rebud on the opposite side; but make the horizontal incision below the level of the original to avoid transection of the bark. With this routine of inspection all stocks enter the winter carrying a living dormant bud, but some losses must be expected if severe weather is prolonged.

At the end of February the entire top growth of the stock is cut off about a quarter of an inch above the bud insertion, using stout secateurs or a fine hacksaw. A 3ft cane is inserted close to the stump, either vertically if neatness matters, or in the direction in which the bud will grow out. From March onwards is an exciting time for the amateur, as he will now scrutinise his stock daily for signs of the swelling of a dark red bud which heralds success. The whole energy of the root system is diverted into the growth of the single inserted bud, but the new growth is soft and as yet inadequately supported by developing woody tissues. Careful tying to the cane with loops of soft wide raffia will give it reasonable support, but it is important to ensure an even tension in successive ties; a violent spring rainstorm can snap the tops of such supple growth. The growing maidens will respond generously to top dressings of manure, compost or peat and fertiliser. By late June the first flower buds will be seen, and they will be in full bloom by mid July. Dead-heading is just as important as with established trees and helps to encourage basal dormant buds to break into secondary shoots. At the end of September, when it is ready for transplanting to a permanent site, an average tree will have a stout original stem and two or three secondary shoots.

With patience, a little practice in taking the bud and an intention to observe and profit from mistakes, this can become a stimulating pastime. I know several novices who obtained 60–70 per cent success at the first attempt and improved to 80–90 per cent in their second year.

BUTCHER'S BROOM   Clarence Elliott

To most people who know the plant only casually, butcher's broom
is a rather dull sort of shrub—and a decidedly spiteful one. One
meets it now and then in shrubberies, and occasionally in the south
of England as a truly wild, woodland plant. Growing two to three
feet high, it forms clumps of erect green stems, with bushy, besom
heads of dark, glossy, oval leaves, tough, leathery and each armed
with a needle-sharp prickle.

As a rule that is about all there is to butcher's broom. It flowers,
but unless you know where to look, and when, you might easily miss
the minute white blossoms, carried almost stemless in the centres
of the holly-hard leaves. Botanically, and theoretically, what we
call the leaves are not true leaves, but 'short leaf-like branches'.
The real leaves, which are below the false leaves, are minute,
almost microscopical scales. But, as gardener to gardener, the
minute flowers are borne in the centres of the leaves, and sometimes they are followed by great scarlet berries. These are quite
twice the size of holly berries and, squatting as they do in the very
centre of a leaf, look suspiciously like a practical joke. Unfortunately, the berries are rare in gardens, for as a rule the plants carry
either all male, pollen-bearing flowers, or all female ones, and
unless one happens to have both a male and a female specimen, the
chances of berries are small.

There is, however, a form of butcher's broom with hermaphrodite flowers: that is to say, flowers with both anthers and
stigmas—and ovaries. They are thus able to produce berries without the presence of another plant of the opposite sex. I had heard
of such a form, but had never had the luck to see it, much less to
possess it, until about a year ago I had a stroke of great good for-
tune. I was motoring along a country road, several miles from
nowhere, when I noticed a roadside dump, on which a quantity of
builders' rubbish had been shot recently, and with it a clump of
butcher's broom. I stopped to investigate and found that, although
the plant was mud-stained and decidedly scruffy, having evidently
led a tough life until it was slung out by the builder, it was carrying
a fine crop of scarlet berries. Without a doubt it was the rare

L   159

hermaphrodite variety, and this was confirmed when I discovered where it had come from: it had been a solitary specimen. This waif, now established in my garden, has already made moderate fresh growth and started to fruit.

Shortly after making that discovery, I met specimens of the hermaphrodite butcher's broom in a neighbour's garden. There were two or three old clumps, and near these several self-sown seedlings, and the youngsters were fruiting as freely as their parents. It looks, therefore, as though this most desirable plant has the happy gift of breeding true to type, though I understand that the raising of seedlings is likely to be a slow, waiting business.

At least one nursery offers the above form as *Ruscus aculeatus Hermaphrodite*.

Ed

PINK LABURNUM   E. M. Blackwell

Our purple-flowered or pink-flowered laburnum bloomed well this year and again surprised visitors who did not know its history. The first of its kind was produced by accident in 1825, when a nurseryman of Vitry near Paris, by name Adam, budded the bushy *Cytisus purpureus* on to laburnum stock, hoping to get thereby a purple broom in tree form. The bud died but later, from the callus formed round the shield, an adventitious bud developed and grew into a shoot bearing leaves smaller than those of the laburnum, without the characteristic silky hairs on the underside. When flowers appeared on the new tree they were of a dingy purple colour on short racemes. The tree was reported as a graft-hybrid and named *Cytisus adami*. As it grew older it produced from the hybrid branches two other types; strong sweeping branches of laburnum with long racemes of yellow flowers, and tufts of the bushybroom with purple flowers in pairs.

Graft-hybrids have since been obtained from other plants: for example, medlar and hawthorn, and potato and tomato; and there is the historic Bizzaria orange which turned up in Florence. But the earlier phenomenon has not been repeated, so that all trees of *C adami* are grafts from the one source on fresh laburnum stock.

Botanists call the plant a periclinal chimaera, as it appears to be built up of the tissues of laburnum shut in by the skin of purple broom. Buds formed from the inner tissues give laburnum shoots, and those formed from skin tissue give shoots of purple broom.

Whereas the yellow and purple flowers are followed by fruits of laburnum and broom respectively and give fertile seeds each of its own kind, the hybrid flowers just wither away. There have been many attempts to induce fruit-formation, but they have met with little success, owing apparently to the inability of the pollen tubes to penetrate the stigma, and not to infertile pollen grains; and the ovules are malformed. One summer some years ago we noticed hybrid pods swelling. Alas, when they were opened we found not seeds but grubs, which were identified as the insect parasite of broom, a species of *Asphondylia*. The 'pod' was a gall due to irritation caused by a sucking grub.

Cytisus adami

A WINTER GARDEN   S. Clapham

My garden has quite a good selection of winter-flowering plants, but I often feel that they are less effective than they might be.

Although most of them are satisfying enough individually, they are dotted all over the place, whereas I would prefer to see them together. In fact, I have often toyed with the idea of transferring some of the younger ones to a winter garden which, I am optimistic enough to think, might be an oasis of colour and fragrance in the bleak grey days. Ideally it would be on the sunny side of an old wall, over which the sulphur-yellow *Forsythia suspensa atrocaulis* would be trained, together with one or two of the so-called japonicas: *Chaenomeles lagenaria* Boule de Feu, with brilliant red flowers, and the pure white *C l nivalis*. All of these flower early in March, so they may fairly be included.

A little way from the wall I would have the winter-flowering cherry *Prunus subhirtella autumnalis*, bespangled from November to March with inch-wide, semi-double flowers, and the pale yellow winter sweet, *Chimonanthus fragrans*, which needs the shelter of a wall to give of its best. Here, too, would be bushes of the creamy-flowered fragrant *Lonicera purpusii*, the sweet-scented *Viburnum fragrans* and also the spidery-bloomed witch-hazel, *Hammamelis mollis*, which I regard as indispensable because, unlike winter sweet which takes several years to bloom, it usually flowers in the first year after planting. Another member of the same family which might be included is the evergreen *Sycopsis sinensis*, a hardy shrub which eventually attains a height of about 7ft and, from February onwards, carries a profusion of small red-and-yellow flowers, each consisting largely of a brush-like bunch of stamens. Its main drawback is that the flowers tend to be hidden by the leaves, but there are usually enough in evidence to provide a quite colourful effect.

In my winter garden all these shrubs would stand on a raised bed; alternatively one part of the ground would be built up and held in place by a retaining wall. Over this *Jasminum nudiflorum* would cascade, for I find that its spraying shoots do not take kindly to wall culture, and here they would have their fling. If the wall faced south I would plant at its foot, in rubbly heaps of soil enriched only with a little lime and bone-meal, the winter-flowering *Iris unguicularis* (*stylosa*). In the gritty, limy soil of the open spaces at the top of the wall would go the early saxifrages of the Kabschia type: the yellow *S apiculata*, pink Cranbourne and grey-leaved, white-flowered *S burseriana*. Admittedly these do not like to be baked in the sun, but they are too precious to omit and can easily be provided with a little shade in our occasional hot summers.

Behind the saxifrages and among the shrubs I would have that most obliging of all winter-flowering plants, *Erica carnea*, the different varieties of which would give good patches of colour from November to April. They would also provide good ground cover for the indispensable *Daphne mezereum*. The less hardy *D odora* would be something of a gamble, but I would be tempted to risk it in a sheltered spot if the soil were lime-free and contained plenty of humus. In addition to the Christmas rose, *Helleborus niger*, I would want to make room for two hellebores: the green-flowered *H corsicus*, with its superb foliage, and the almost equally decorative *H foetidus*, with its red-tipped green flowers in early spring.

Last and by no means least I would group bulbs and corms boldly to give plenty of colour. Scillas, snowdrops, chionodoxas, crocuses (including the early *C sieberi*, *C imperati* and *C korolkowi*) should present no difficulty. The same cannot be said of the winter-flowering *C orbiculatum coum* (*C coum* in some catalogues), but I would try a patch of it in a shady corner where there is plenty of humus and some lime. To forestall the main display of daffodils, the 3in high *Narcissus minimus* and the taller *N cyclamineus* might also be included.

This, then, would be my choice for a winter garden; but, alas, it would require a lot of room and some patience where the shrubs were concerned. Meanwhile I am planting any new winter-flowering acquisitions together in one place.

THE WHITTY PEAR   Augusta Paton

In 1962 a single true service tree, whitty pear or sorb, *Sorbus domestica* was found growing on the edge of a wood in Worcestershire. It produces flowers and fruit but, though a beautiful specimen, is by no means fully grown, being a little less than forty feet high with a girth, at three and a half feet, of fifty inches. Its neighbours in the thicket are typical lime-loving trees and shrubs: ash, maple, dogwood, guelder-rose and privet. Not far away grow oak, spindle, butterfly orchid, hound's-tongue, dropwort and four kinds of wild rose. Nightingales sing there in spring.

How did the tree get there? The only other known wild-growing whitty pear was the famous one in the Wyre Forest first mentioned by Edmund Pitt, an alderman of Worcester, in 1678 and maliciously burnt in 1862. Saplings from it were successfully propagated by the Woodwards of Arley Castle, and one was planted at the original site by Mrs Woodward in 1916. Today it is about the same size as its new rival and produces fruit, though not every year. An inscription below commemorates its ancestry. Other descendants were planted at the Precentory in Worcester and, recently, near the Chapter House. One at the Oxford Botanic Garden is said to have been planted about 1790 from fruit gathered in the Wyre Forest. Two others, at Croome Court, almost certainly came from Arley stock and, though they are now no more, it seems possible that bird-sown seed from one of them gave rise to the recently discovered tree.

The true service tree is a native of the continent of Europe, and it is most unlikely that the original specimen was indigenous. An examination of its surroundings about a hundred years ago showed traces of a dwelling; and the most probable explanation is that the young tree was planted by a forest keeper at a time when this country had close connexions with France.

The species resembles the rowan or mountain ash, except that its leaves are more downy beneath and the clusters of berries not so flat. The greatest difference lies in the fruits, which are like small bunches of green pears, tinged with yellow on one side when ripe; they are harsh and astringent but, when kept until October, have the same pleasant acidity as medlars. In Anjou and in central and southern Europe the fruit was used to make a kind of wine or perry; and the tree was cultivated for its wood, which is very hard, takes a high polish and was much sought after by turners and cabinetmakers. It was also used for mill machinery and musical instruments. The rowan was deemed to have protective powers, and the sorb was supposed to be even more efficacious. The dried fruit was hung in cottages to keep witches away and, even in 1867, the idea of its virtues had not entirely died out.

In the West Country the rowan was locally known as the whitty, wicken or quicken tree; and 'whitty pear' means simply the rowan with pear-like fruit. 'Whitty' may be derived from the Anglo-Saxon *witan*, meaning knowledge or wisdom, with reference to the tree as a charm. Another name is cheque tree, possibly from 'choker'—an allusion to the unpalatable fruit.

The original tree, described in detail and illustrated by Nash in his *History of Worcestershire* in 1781, had become a withered wreck by the middle of the last century, although the top branches still bore flowers and fruit at their extremities (see picture on page 90). It was destroyed by a poacher who had been sentenced by a local magistrate, Squire Childe of Kinlet, with a particular liking for the tree. The blackened stump and limbs were collected by a Bewdley botanist who had four goblets made from the branches; a bench of its wood was presented to the Hastings Museum in Worcester but has now disappeared, and two boxes were made by the foresters.

HERBACEOUS BORDERS IN THE WIND
Mary Horsbrugh Porter

Gardeners who live on hillsides and in other exposed positions have a definite enemy in the form of wind. Still days are the exception, not the rule, and unless the garden has a high wall or protective hedges to act as wind-breaks much damage is done to tall plants and those with brittle stems, especially just before and during their flowering peak. So if we live well above sea level and wish to own a herbaceous border we must sacrifice the tall plants if we are to avoid the disappointment and frustration of seeing the border after a summer gale. Staking prevents some of this destruction by keeping the flower stems from breaking but does not always prevent a windswept appearance, nor a twisted distorted effect; and for me a heavily staked border loses much of its natural charm. All this and more I discovered when I came to live up on the Cotswolds where the soil and position could not have been more different from the turf loam and shelter of my old-fashioned garden within high red brick walls in southern Ireland. As compensation I found that there was a large choice of bushy herbaceous plants and dwarf varieties, so that once my low-growing border was established I would have few regrets.

In place of tall delphiniums I discovered the belladonnas, which do not exceed 2ft or 3ft and have wiry stems, as does the dwarf delphinium Tom Thumb, which is a real gentian blue. So I did not have to deny myself those drifts of blue so essential to the midsummer border. Thus encouraged I began to look round the gardens of others, taking special note of any plants that looked suitable for my new border. One of the earliest discoveries was buphthalmum, a very fascinating little golden-yellow daisy which is lowgrowing and flowers almost continuously from June till the end of August; the few pieces I was originally given made neat round plants the following year, well suited to their position towards the front of the border. Aquilegias, always a great standby during the early summer, were a great success, for not only were the stems wiry and wind-resistant but the foliage remained attractive long after the dead flower-heads had been cut off; the grace of the blooms and the variety of their colours were a joy for several weeks. The same was true of the pyrethrums, whose lovely pinks and reds made a brave show in the later days of June and in July. Moreover, both had blooms to spare for indoor decoration—an important function of the border.

The vivid blue cranesbill becomes rather windswept but has advantages that outweigh this. The colour is just right to show off the orange of *Erigeron aurantiacus* and the silveriness of *Stachys lanata*, so like lambs' ears, by which name the more common variety is known. Besides when the time comes to cut off the dead heads, one is left with a neat compact clump of green foliage which turns red in the autumn. Catmint, a border favourite, has none of these qualities, and I resolved to banish it for its untidy sprawling habits and far from fragrant smell. *Campanula carpatica* is far better for the front of the border, its bluebell-like flowers continuing from June till late August; and beside it I could not resist planting that old-fashioned border pink, Mrs Sinkins, in both pink and white. Tidy she is not, but her scent on a still summer's evening is a just recompense.

For a year or two, until the border was full of perennials and entirely to my satisfaction, I included dwarf varieties of antirrhinums and sweet williams, for I felt that these would be more in keeping with the rest. Pentstemons, both blue and red, I found invaluable for midsummer and later flowering: not only were they long-lasters but they had that little extra height which breaks the line in this type of border. Anthemis, too, has this special advantage, and it is wiry-stemmed; it colours the border for weeks with three different and equally good shades of yellow.

Among autumn plants I place michaelmas daisies high in the herbaceous stakes. The dwarf and low-growing varieties are charming and of many different shades which add blue, mauve and red to the colour scheme. The autumn border needs to be of deep rich hues to tone with the season's vivid and distinctive colours. For this reason I was keen to include the dahlias Bishop of Llandaff and Grenadier for their attractive red foliage and vivid red flowers, which are perfect against the blues and mauves of michaelmas daisies and the orange and red of rudbeckias, in particular the one we call Black-eyed Susan, a lovely low-growing autumn flower. To make the dahlias conform in height I had to stop all early buds, thus encouraging a more bushy habit. Then there were the sedums, and how I blessed their unconcerned air of prosperity during the long drought! There are two shades of *Sedum spectabile*, one pale pink and the other a brilliant carmine; and the fleshy leaves, the secret of their drought-resisting propensities, are distinctive at all seasons. I never found chrysanthemums suitable as border plants until I was presented with a fascinating little pale pink pom-pom which was only about a foot high. Another, sent by a nurseryman in place of one he could not supply, turned out to be a gem, and Jewel was indeed its name; the not-so-small flowers were a pretty brick red with a yellow centre, and its full height not more than 9in.

There are, of course, a great many other plants suitable for this type of border, but when planning there are a few points to keep in mind. It is all-important to have the border filled to capacity, for this not only discourages weeds but lessens wind damage, because the plants protect each other. Big bold splashes of colour are effective because they fill the eye, and the art of successful border gardening is to have as much colour as possible at all times throughout the season. So plant generously and avoid a patchy appearance. Above all, do not have a uniform pattern of tall plants at the back and small ones at the front; avoid the rigid lines that look unnatural.

I discovered, too, that there are advantages as well as disadvantages about gardens on hillsides. They do not usually suffer from late spring and early autumn frosts, which form pockets in the valleys and do untold harm. Nor do plants damp off on high ground, where the drainage is good and soil light. Damp kills far more precious plants every winter than cold, and high ground, though it may be cold, is dry. Last but not least of the advantages is a view. What better background is there for the colour of a flower garden than an English landscape?

STARTING MISTLETOE   E.D.W.

For starting mistletoe it is essential to have a ripe berry. Mistletoe berries are fully ripe in February and March, and it will therefore be useless to try to perpetuate Christmas souvenirs. The method is simple, as is well known. Make a slight cut in the bark at a young joint. Do this on the under side, so that birds cannot get at the seed. Slightly raise the bark on each side of the cut, crush the berry, and gently push in the seed with some of the juicy flesh adhering. The bark should then be firmly pressed down again to close the cut, and must be covered with gauze or muslin. Germination is slow, and, during the first year, only two small leaves will sprout. Once the growth is established the plant becomes hardy and will stand any climate.

WHY COOK VEGETABLES?   Eleanour Sinclair Rohde

How very odd to cook vegetables! Raw vegetables (properly prepared, of course) are more digestible, more appetising and far more healthgiving than dead stuff deprived of nearly all its best qualities.

Certain vegetables, notably peas and beans, artichokes and starchy vegetables such as potatoes and parsnips have to be cooked, but why cook cauliflowers, any of the green vegetables, or roots? Many of these require no cooking and are far better in every way eaten raw.

Green vegetables are still usually boiled in large quantities of water in spite of the fact that the salts of all green vegetables are soluble. Further, boiled greens are extremely indigestible, and their taste unless well disguised is just horrid and sloppy. Thousands of people eat boiled cabbage and similar horrors from a sense of duty. They cannot possibly like such stuff, and no wonder it is difficult to persuade children to eat the vegetables put before them. The maltreated vegetables are merely what dieticians call roughage, but it is so well disguised in expensive restaurants that most people do not realise they are eating rubbish. Eat root vegetables and greens raw and you will wonder why you ever tolerated the nonsense of cooking them.

Take, for instance, the vegetables in season now. Broccoli, like cauliflowers or for that matter any of the numerous edible flowers, are most wholesome and perfectly digestible if eaten raw. Cooked, they taste what they are, dead; and they are notoriously indigestible. To prepare these heads to perfection, gather them not a moment before they are required and wash them well, first in salted and then fresh water. Then grate as finely as possible. Broccoli and cauliflowers grate to a powdery consistency. Fill cup-like lettuce leaves, or orange skins cut in half, with the grated vegetable and cover with mayonnaise sauce. Or mix the vegetable with finely chopped herbs such as sweet marjoram, thyme, a very little sage, lovage, chives and so forth.

Brussels sprouts, firm savoys and cabbages also grate to a powdery yet moist consistency. There are special machines for mincing vegetables finely, and it is sometimes easier to use them minced than to grate by hand. We usually find it necessary to put greens twice through a mincer. Carrots grated raw, especially mature specimens, which are sweet, are delicious. They should never be peeled. Turnips also are good when grated but, unlike carrots, usually have to be peeled. Incidentally, townsfolk seem to like young root vegetables, another of their odd likes, for these immature roots are poor in flavour and as unwholesome as unripe fruits.

The rarely grown Hamburgh parsley, which makes large edible roots, grates to the same consistency as ground nuts and has a delicious nutty flavour. Onions grate well, but they can be used only as a flavouring in a dish of mixed vegetables as the flavour is so strong. Cucumber and vegetable marrow grate and help to moisten rather dry roots such as radishes.

Mixed raw vegetables make a more interesting dish than vegetables served separately. Green and root vegetables blend admirably, and the greater the mixture the better. Failing mayonnaise sauce, a little cream is a good addition. There are numerous methods of serving grated raw vegetables but they look best, I think, as I have said, served in individual portions in small lettuce leaves, or in orange skins halved or even in tiny ornamental gourds with the pulp scooped out. We find that all mixtures are greatly improved by a judicious addition of herbs, especially sweet herbs such as lavender—it is odd how few people realise that the leaves are edible—rosemary, sweet cicely, lovage, southernwood, angelica leaf, dill, thyme and so forth.

THE BLEEDING VINE   S.C.B.

An old inhabitant said that he reckoned the wall that carried my vine wor about a hundred year old as far as he did know. Anyhow, the vine worn't no good, and never had been. The bole is fourteen inches round, and the vine is stopped at fourteen foot, because the gardener thinks that is a pretty height, and he can't reach no further. It was pruned to eight rods, the eighth laced with branches from the large blue plum. To cut one rod from eight would hardly hurt the vine—it would not matter if it did.

I cut the rod at a point where it was one and a half inches in diameter. The sap oozed out in a steady trickle.

'Heat the poker red hot,' I said to the gardener, 'and rub it on the cut.' He did this, but the bleeding continued.

'Heat the poker again, and bring a candle. We will seal the cut with hot wax.'

This proved useless, so we tried sealing wax. The wax stuck well, but the vine still bled. It was beginning to look as though the poor old vine would bleed to death. I decided to ring a friend who goes in for grapes. He would know what to do.

'I've cut a branch of my vine, and it's bleeding to death.'

'What! at this time of year! Heavens, I don't know. Get a large potato, cut it in half, scoop out a hole and press firmly on the cut.'

I found a whopper, a good four inches wide, and pressed it on until my arms began to ache. By now it was almost dark, but sap was still oozing from the bark at some inches below the cut. Oh, well—it was a silly thing to do. The poor old vine would just have to die.

Next morning I found a saturated patch of blackened earth a foot across. The vine must have bled a bucketful, and the bleeding from under the potato was as free as ever. I put a bucket underneath and later in the day I found this was nearly full. I tipped out the sap and put the bucket back. About a week later the sap was still dropping. It took weeks to stop, and I do not know how many bucketfuls the vine bled, but it was not less than four. I had lost interest, for the vine would soon be dead.

Yet in spring the buds began to break. They came on strong and showed no signs of dying. I used the sulphur bellows, and in the fine hot summer the vine did well. I dressed it again with sulphur and thinned out the bunches.

'What!' said the old inhabitant, 'a hundred pound o' grapes off that ole vine!—and bunches weighing a pound? It never bore no fruit worth thinkin' on so far as I did know!'

'Ah!' I replied loftily, 'but that was because of those old-fashioned gardeners!'

PLANTING A TREE

The future, with earthy roots, is in my hands,
Bursting with promise of long leafy years
When my own promise, barren or fulfilled,
Shall call no more for triumph or for tears.

This sapling is a bridge from mind to mind,
To that changed world where I should lose my way,
For there, beneath its shadow, men may think
The thoughts I planted, planting it today.

Violet Latham

TAIL CORN

Gardener, extracting a wriggling worm from his fork and popping it into his mouth with relish: 'That's the best way with worms. They does you a power o' good and gets rid of 'em for good an all.'

Index